The Educational Enclave

Coercive Bargaining in Colleges and Universities

The Educational Enclave

✸✸✸ Coercive Bargaining in Colleges

and Universities ✸✸ *by Norman Matlin*

FUNK & WAGNALLS, NEW YORK

Contents

The Educational Enclave

Coercive Bargaining in Colleges and Universities

Introduction

When I began to write my thesis on education, from which this book has finally emerged, I read a number of works on education. Despite the fact that the authors disagreed violently with each other, and occasionally with themselves, the books showed a rather depressing degree of similarity. However loud the argument, the authors seemed in fundamental agreement with other educators that educational institutions are set up to teach, that they have, to some degree, fallen short of this noble ideal, and that something should be done posthaste. The various suggestions as to what ought to be done tended to cancel each other out, except for a general feeling that more money ought to be spent.

My own background is in the social sciences rather than in education. I assume that educators, in reading the literature in their field, are not as repelled as I was. The social sciences are by no means free of exhortatory literature. Nonetheless, it is rare that a book purporting to be social science is written exclusively in this vein. At the least, lip service is given to the notion that a description of the existing world is a starting point for an analysis of a situation.

In fact, in some of the disciplines of social science, such as anthropology, it is fashionable to assume that the function of anything will differ from the participants' description of it. Of course, the anthropologist has the advantage of dealing with natives, who can hardly be expected to understand what they are about. Nevertheless, the practice of assuming institutions to be guided by latent functions is widespread in the analyses of our own society. Analyses of the functioning of organizations solely in terms of their avowed ends is considered somewhat unsophisticated, even gauche.

This is not to say that starting out from the conviction that all men are liars, as some of the works of social science do, necessarily makes you any less likely to be fooled. But it does tend to throw the burden of proof onto a description of how institutions work and to make their actions the touchstone for evaluating their words. It requires no great commitment to cynicism to predict that some startling discrepancies between actions and words will be found. These discrepancies are also apparent in the literature of education. The peculiar flavor of educational literature, however, arises from a tendency to take the words as given and to proceed to an analysis of why actions, which should follow logically from these words, have not occurred. The approach of social science would be to try to understand actions and infer from them the function of educational institutions. In practice, social scientists rarely take so inductive an approach. After looking about a bit, they set up a plausible theoretical system, make some deductions from it, and try to investigate the actual situation to evaluate to what degree the real world corresponds to their predictions.

Further consideration of the literature of education led me to the conclusion that its idiosyncrasies are not merely stylistic, but result from a platonic notion of the world, generally abandoned by the social sciences in the late Middle Ages. I will enlarge somewhat on the implications of this understanding of the world in later discussion.

I intended in my thesis to sketch out a model for education that would follow in general outline the model of the marketplace of the classical economists. Anthony Downs' model of democratic government has demonstrated the fruitfulness of the application of economic thinking to spheres outside those conventionally assigned to economists. Although my model was designed to predict in general terms the course of education, it was not designed to cover every exigency or explain every paradox. At points it was necessary, however, to cite the situation in the real world as a check that the model had not gone off on a completely wild tack. In the course of this periodic reference to reality, some anomalies of education which presented problems for the model were gone into in perhaps greater detail than were originally intended.

In no sense of the word was the thesis or the subsequent volume intended as an experimental study. Thus the careful methodological considerations appropriate to empirical studies largely did not apply. The reader has been spared a host of irrelevant citations. Even had I been so minded, circumstances would have sharply limited the number of references. Since the theory sketched out departs at several places from the conventional theories, it points to classes of phenomena that have largely been ignored in the literature of education, since they have not fitted easily into the usual framework. Recourse has had to be taken at many points to facts that are matters of common knowledge, although they would never be discovered by reading about education.

Although my thesis earned me my degree, my argument fared rather more poorly. I found it advisable, about halfway through the work, to pay attention to the power relationships between various groups on the campus. The economic model that I had adopted made no provision for such relationships. I had recourse to a series of more conventional sociological concepts which served the purpose fairly adequately.

The result, therefore, while descriptively respectable, was aesthetically infelicitous. I could find no harmonious way to link two sets of concepts, each of which individually provided an adequate framework for explaining certain aspects of the workings of educational institutions.

I put aside any further work on educational institutions, devoting myself to various and sundry activities involved in making a living. Rather unsystematic observations of other institutions in our society suggested to me that the understanding of these institutions ran into similar difficulties. Economists, on the one hand, and sociologists, on the other, studying the same complex, seem to come up with analyses hardly recognizable as describing the same institution. Nonetheless, many of these analyses seem quite reasonable as far as they go. The situation appears to me to call for a framework able to integrate the partial insights of the economic model and the power model.

Relationships in the world in which we live seem to be conducted in a fashion that is not quite so free as the free marketplace postulated by the classic liberals, nor yet so completely power-oriented as the political model favored by the sociologists. Most transactions seem to be conducted under the influence of a moderate degree of coercion. Yet the rules by which such bargaining would be conducted have never been developed. While isolated studies of particular situations have taken cognizance of the mixed nature of the transactions they are studying, I have found no one, in my exceedingly casual perusal of the literature, who attempts to articulate concepts that will be broadly applicable for a series of different types of transactions.

In this work I attempt to suggest some concepts generally usable for the study of societal institutions. In the absence of any accepted terminology for the situations with which I am trying to deal, I have cheerfully invented my own vocabulary. Although I believe these concepts to be fruitful in many areas, I have restrained myself to their use in understanding educational institutions. The successful application of concepts designed to be general to a particular situation is the best recommendation for essaying their use in other contexts.

Chapter 1 considers the general nature of current theory in education and the social sciences. I attempt to examine various theories that might form the basis for an understanding of educational institutions and evaluate their utility for this purpose. I there expand considerably the argumentation that I have only adumbrated here.

Chapter 2 sketches out the general theory of coercive bargaining which I feel is necessary to bridge the gap between economic theory and sociological theory.

Chapter 3 evaluates the utility of this theory with the interpretation of education and begins a general analysis of educational institutions in these terms. The following seven chapters are devoted to various aspects of education as it can be understood in terms of the theory of coercive bargaining; the concluding chapter reexamines the status of standard educational theory.

No doubt the reader will trace in this work the influence of the classic economists, Anthony Downs, James S. Duesenberry, and Thorstein Veblen. For me to attempt to complement these writers would be the height of presumption.

I wish to express my especial gratitude to Doctor Arthur J. Vidich, whose encouragement and aid made this theoretical exercise possible, and to Doctor Dennis H. Wrong and Doctor Bernard Rosenberg, who showed commendable forebearance as members of my committee. I am indebted also to Anne Handschu, subsequently Anne Handschu Matlin, whose help was invaluable, and to Barry Bernard Levine, whose irritating criticisms contributed greatly to its logical rigor.

Naturally, none of the people who have knowingly or unknowingly contributed to the writing of this study can be held responsible for the errors of omission or commission contained therein; the faults are mine.

N. M.

1

Preliminary Skirmishes

This is a rather unusual book about education. Along with other peculiarities, it discusses in large part the nature of society rather than the field of education. Given my own particular view of the world as one in which societies spin off a number of semiautonomous enclaves, the structures of which are governed by the conditions of their generation, the peculiar construction of the book is understandable, perhaps even appropriate. The conditions of the surrounding world must be taken into consideration if we are to understand the nature of the educational enclave. I hope that the discussion of education as an example of a semiautonomous quasi-society will encourage, in addition to clarification of the nature of the educational enclave, further analysis along the same line of other enclaves.

It is traditional for an author, before he begins the exposition of his own theoretical system, to consider a number of other systems and explain his reasons for rejecting them as inadequate frameworks for his study. The more astute reader recognizes that the underlying reason for the rejection of all other systems is the author's desire to develop his own. I am undoubtedly guilty of similar self-serving motives. Nevertheless, everybody's theories, my own included, are subject to a plethora of limitations, being of necessity simplified models of a complex world. The particular limitations that I have chosen to stress in other people's ideas will serve to inform the reader of the reasoning behind the development of my system and perhaps will make up for the casual style of my own exposition.

Let us begin our consideration of possible theories with the standard educational theory. This theory assumes that students want to learn, that they attend universities in order to learn more, and that they take their leave of the university when they have learned as much as they are able. If they are fortunate enough to have the capacity to assimilate a full four-year dose of knowledge, they leave with a diploma attesting to the fact. The faculty and administration are motivated by the desire to impart knowledge, dedicating their lives, their fortunes, and their sacred honor to this never-ending, but eternally satisfying, task.

This is, of course, a shortened version of the common denominator of numerous complicated educational explanations. The basic assumptions of standard educational theory are rarely presented so baldly, perhaps never outside graduation day oratory. In longer and more sympathetic presentations, the attribution of the motivation to learn, to students, and the motivation to teach, to professors, is usually hedged with some more or less ill-tempered criticism of the varying actors for having fallen short of the motivations attributed to them. In general, the awareness of the lamentable failure to cooperate fully with the hypothesized attitudes is rarely carried into the subsequent analysis. It remains conveniently accessible to explain those aspects of educational practice that the particular theorist does not favor. The bulk of educational behavior remains to be understood in terms of the basic motivations.

We must, of course, be careful not to draw any naively erroneous conclusions from the postulated motivations. Faculty and administrators are not usually independently wealthy; they cannot afford, however generous they may be, to donate their services gratis, but must expect that their labors will yield them enough to eat and to support their families. Nor, indeed, should this stipend be the bare minimum, but should be ample to support the teacher in accordance with his station in life.

Even with this emendation, the foregoing may appear to be a rather slender base for the complex calculations that are needed in any large-scale educational discussion. As a matter of fact, however, virtually all theories turn out to be analyzable to a small number of basic assumptions.

These few are highly practical. Summing the teachers' salaries, adding the fixed expenses for buildings, laboratories, and other academic equipment, we arrive at the total cost of the educational enterprise. The total cost, minus the amounts available from philanthropic sources, governmental or private, gives the amount to be contributed by students. This latter amount, divided by the number of students, gives the tuition.

It is, of course, interesting to know whether these calculations produce figures that are actually descriptive of prices in the educational field. At the present time I doubt that they are able to do so without a good deal of "rigging." In all probability, however, calculations of this sort were at one time highly predictive of prices. What is even more theoretically interesting is the question of why theories predict well when they do. To explore this question we shall have to examine the nature of theory.

In the natural sciences, we tend to find necessary theories. The theory is a set of abstractions developed to predict data. It can be conceptualized as simply descriptive, a basically shorthand way of summarizing in a few general principles the regularities to be found in information. The development of the theory, per se, has no effect on the data it is designed to explain. If I understand why chemical X combines with chemical Y to produce chemical Z, this does not in any way affect the reaction. I do not have to worry that chemical X will read the theory and come to the conclusion that it had better act this way. The theory lives in a separate world.

Within the social sciences, on the other hand, this preoccupation is the standard state of affairs. People read the theory and, if it strikes them as correct, act as the theory said they were acting all the time. Theory in the social sciences is contingent, not necessary.

The task of proving a theory in the social sciences is thus somewhat paradoxical. I may articulate a theory that is not at all descriptive of the fact at the time that I articulate it. If it becomes popular, the facts change to meet my theory. I am then in a position to say "I told you so." Much of the success of psychologists and other faith healers depends on this circular process.

This does not necessarily mean that the theorist had this in mind when he published his theory. He may have been sincerely attempting to give an accurate description of the way things were. If anything, this is likely to improve his chances of making them that way. If the theory turns out to be normative, it may be so precisely because it is seen as merely descriptive.

I am aware that this description of the nature of the social sciences is a controversial one. Many, if not most, modern social scientists do not consider the social sciences as intrinsically different from the natural sciences. The theories generated by what we may loosely term the behaviorists are patterned on theories in the natural sciences. Much of their success derives from their publication.

It may be pointed out, however, that insofar as these theories become normative, they are accepted not because this is the way things ought to be but because this is the way they are believed to be. The argument is putatively empiric rather than ethical. It may be considered both the strength and the weakness of standard economic theory that it is simultaneously both a picture of the way things ought to be and a description of the way things are. Its normative base is not merely empirical, but ethical.

Given the analysis of the social sciences sketched above, it is obvious that an ethical theory may well be highly descriptive of the information it attempts to explain. The mere fact that a theorist is committed to the vision of a perfect world does not mean that the world he describes may not be at least approximately perfect. The possibility may become clearer if we look at another theory with a basically similar structure: medieval economic theory.[1] *

The medieval economists assumed that manufacturers were in business in order to provide the public with their wares. Nonetheless, however basically altruistic the manufacturer's intention, he was entitled to some compensation for his wares. His selling price could be calculated by adding to his costs the amount of profit that would enable him to live in reasonable comfort. This was known as the just price. It was readily calculable, in theory, although there was usually a fair degree of argument about its calculation in practice.

Present-day notions of the *raison d'être* of the manufacturer are sufficiently different from medieval concepts that it is easy to see that the medieval economist began with an analysis of the manufacturer's obligations to society and proceeded with the assumption that prices would be fixed by that obligation. In more modern terms, we would say that the economist confused function with motivation.

Nevertheless, the medieval economist's formulations, no matter how odd the logic by which he arrived at them, did predict prices in the Middle Ages. In fact, they predicted prices far better than would more modern theories applied to the medieval situation. We cannot legitimately conclude that a theory, just because it starts from moral assumptions, does not accurately predict practice.

We may, however, ask under what conditions it is likely to be an accurate index of an actual situation. Certainly, if all the people involved in the interaction being studied are committed, in their conduct as well as verbally, to the moral principles assumed in the theory, we may expect, if the theory is physically possible, that the predictions will be accurate. In fact, it is hardly necessary that complete unanimity exist. If the bulk of the people are committed, we may expect that the predictions will work pretty well.

While an occasional deviate is not enough to upset a theory, the success of a number of persons who do not subscribe to the

* Superscript numerals refer to Notes (see pp. 219–222).

moral principles of the community may attract attention and provide for others the temptation to emulate their irresponsibility. In the absence of any hindrance, a system based on moral codes may rapidly run downhill. In fact, as was noted by Machiavelli in the sixteenth century, moral codes which work in practice turn out to have been backed by force.

The tendency of medieval merchants and manufacturers to settle on a just price was less a tribute to their commitment to the moral principles postulated by the economist than to the generous help given them by guild and government in avoiding mathematical error.

Thus, the concept of contingency in the social sciences turns out to be somewhat complex. Action may be contingent on belief, but belief is not necessarily a democratic process; some people's beliefs are more important than other people's. It turns out that if we want to have any good idea of how action is governed, we must find out not only what most people believe, but also how the social structure outside our particular sphere of action is functioning.

We will, therefore, have to consider standard educational theory as a limiting case, likely to be true only in selected historical circumstances. It will be predictive only in a given climate of opinion and given a social structure conducive to that opinion. Although it is true that educational discussions today still cling to the rhetoric of standard educational theory, observations of day-to-day decisions made in the educational field do not lead one to the conclusion that the climate of opinion that would make standard educational theory accurately descriptive exists. Nor does the present social structure seem to be committed to the maintenance of anything beyond the most stylistically formalized adherence to the concepts involved.

An explanation of the way in which educational institutions work in modern society must look for a more generalized formulation than that provided by standard educational theory. Hopefully, the theory that we are looking for will provide an explanation not only of how modern educational institutions work but also will suggest why different educational patterns prevail in different circumstances; it will then sketch out the conditions under which a system more or less like that postulated by standard educational theory would function.

In the development of the social sciences since the Middle Ages, there have been two major models used to explain large-scale human behavior: the economic model and the power model. Let us examine each of these and attempt to assess its suitability as an explanation for the conduct of educational institutions.

The classic formulation of the economic model is found in Adam Smith's *The Wealth of Nations*.[2] This model is essentially simple. Man in his economic behavior is motivated by the desire to maximize the amount of goods. Thus, he will buy as cheaply as he can and sell as dearly. Prices are thus set by the law of supply and demand, since the seller will demand as high a price as he can get and the buyer will trade at the lowest price he can find. The existence of a perfect market, of course, requires a number of impossible conditions such as perfect communication and the inability of any particular trade to have any significant effect on the market. Nevertheless, in many areas, practice approximated the perfect model. In 1776, when *The Wealth of Nations* was first published, many businessmen still thought in terms of medieval economic concepts and Adam Smith's description was quite far from being accurate. As the concepts in more simplified form became popular, the market came more and more to resemble Adam Smith's picture of it. This may seem to be giving an undue weight to the social effect of what is, after all, a fairly abstract theory. Capitalist theory necessitated a complete reversal in moral evaluation, however.

For the medieval economist, the hero is the man who foregoes the opportunity to make a fast buck, restraining himself to the limited profit possible under a just price. The villain is the man who sits up nights figuring out how to squeeze every last penny out of each transaction. This dichotomy supplies the standard guide for measuring the moral condition of neighbors.

In Adam Smith, the roles are reversed. The hero is precisely the man most assiduously dedicated to maximizing profit. The merchant who fails to take the utmost advantage of his transactions is not only a fool, a morally neutral figure, but also a villain. In his precipitate haste to aid his fellow man, he is, in fact, retarding the development of the economy and postponing the day when all men will have enough to eat. For a person brought up in medieval economic thought, Smith's analysis is truly the work of the devil.

Lest the description of this reversal be taken as too extreme, look at the history of a similar reversal in our own day.[3] The more elderly among us will remember when Adam Smith's hero was still a model of virtue and the savior of the State. Respectability involved not only maximizing profit, but also saving the result, either for personal investment or for the bank to invest. Among people of worldly success, it was a point of honor not to touch capital. To live beyond your means was scandalous.

Keynesian economics completely reversed the cast of characters. The heretofore model citizen is blamed by Keynes as the father of depressions. His unwillingness to spend his money as fast as he can earn it is considered an inhibition in the turnover of currency which, if it is severe enough, ends up sending his fellow citizens to the breadlines. The Keynesian hero, per contra, is the scapegrace who not only spends his money directly he gets it, but goes out and borrows more in the optimistic prospect that he will somehow find a way to repay it. Thus, the profligate, so long denounced from pulpit and textbook, is seen as the savior of the State and the epitome of good business practice. It was this reversal of roles, rather than any mathematical flaw in Keynesian logic, that accounted for the chilly reception of his theories. Only, in fact, when the business cycle proved totally uncontrollable in conventional terms was Keynesian theory considered seriously. The revolution in moral values that the adoption of Keynesian theory necessitated has taken place within a few short years. The younger generation cannot begin to fathom why anybody would want to save money. However, back to classical economic theory.

Much of the charm of an economic model lies in its paradoxical conclusion that vast numbers of people, interested only in benefiting themselves, succeed in their interaction in benefiting each other. The entire system rests on the regular appearance of unplanned-for benefits. Working within a framework which assumed that benefits had to be planned if they were to appear, Adam Smith took great pains to delineate the conditions under which the invisible hand of the marketplace would work for the maximum benefit. For the marketplace to function efficiently, it was necessary that the government, on the one hand, guarantee the sanctity of contract and break up conspiracies in restraint of trade and, on the other hand, keep its nose out of business. Among other things, it is a tribute to Adam Smith's ability as an advocate that classical economic theory was seriously tried for several decades.

Despite the fact that economic theory called for altruistic and somewhat self-contradictory action on the part of the government, it was considerably less normative than medieval theory. In Smith's own pungent phrasing, "It is not to the generosity of the butcher and the baker that we owe our daily bread, but to their sense of self-interest." Classical economists felt, rather reasonably, that people would continue to believe in their own self-interest without the need for any substantial amount of societal policing.

The difficulty with classical economic theory, and perhaps the cause of its downfall, was its naive assumption that governments could be depended on to act altruistically, even when people did not. This is, in fact, a compound of two assumptions. It assumes, first, that the ends of a State are different from those of an individual, the State being motivated to benefit other people, while individuals are motivated to benefit themselves. Even if we were to accept this notion of the appropriate motivation for government, the State, as a fictitious entity, needs must work through individuals. Since economic theory has previously described individuals as essentially motivated by self-interest, we would expect that the members of the bureaucracy, at every level, would cooperate with State policy only to the degree that it happened to serve their own interest. This analysis would lead us to predict that the government's own bureaucracy would end up by subverting the government's intentions. Yet classic economic theory makes no such assumption. It acts as if the mere employment of a person in a governmental post were sufficient to change his motivation. Not only is the government altruistic but its servants share in this inhuman propensity. It appears, then, that the economic model falls into a slightly more sophisticated version of the trap that it recognizes in medieval economics.

Since Adam Smith, the history of economics has been an attempt to replace his assumptions with a series that could accomplish what he set out to do. Despite the virtual unanimity among economists in the inadequacy of Smith's formulation, there is hardly a shred of agreement about what should be used to replace it.

Although classical economics did not achieve its ends, it did succeed in elucidating a number of concepts. The notion of a bargain as a trade that occurs to the mutual benefit of both parties turns out to be useful in many areas of the social sciences. The calculation of the price at which a bargain will be struck, while again a limiting case, offers a standard for the evaluation of a bargain. The real difficulty in applying the economic model to transactions in real life is the model's assumption that both partners to the bargain are equivalent. In the process of removing all non-economic factors from consideration, the classical economists have created a model that is too far abstracted from the situation in real life to be very helpful. How, in fact, is a bargain struck between two people when one is powerful and the other is weak? The expected non-economic factors will come into play. But the economist has so concentrated on the economic factors as to leave us with no idea whatsoever of how non-economic factors function in an economic transaction. What makes this lacuna so serious is that the entire structure of economic thought depends on the existence of a government whose considerations are not primarily economic.

Once again we must look for a more general theory to account for human conduct. Again we may consider economic theory a limiting case, likely to be predictive only in special circumstances. Hopefully, here again, our theory will be able to specify at least the general nature of the circumstances in which economic behavior will appear.

The other theory with some claim to generality in the social sciences is power theory. This theory has never been articulated with anything like the clarity that Adam Smith gave to economic theory. Numbers of political scientists and sociologists have used the main assumptions of power theory; each has added to it his own particular slant. The description that follows is, of necessity, an impressionistic estimate of the common elements among authors who speak of power.

The theory assumes the basic motivation of man to be the maximization of power, that is, the ability of a person to determine the behavior of other people regardless of their consent. In the final analysis, all power rests on force. For various reasons, however, ruling by pure force is impractical except in such limited cases as family groups. The distribution of physical prowess among adults is relatively equal. Certainly some men are stronger than others. But few men would be able to withstand the combined assault of even a dozen opponents. Thus, natural equipment has imposed a limitation on the extent of domination by sheer physical force.

The ever inventive mind of man has developed numerous technological aids to upset this natural balance. The most conspicuous of these is known, paradoxically, as the equalizer. The use of weapons, however, is also subject to limitations. They are too destructive. The overzealous use of force leaves one in the position of the Roman emperor who created a desert and called it peace. One cannot hope to enjoy the services of a follower after one has killed him.

Short of the ultimate recourse, power has rested on the threat of force. This has certain obvious advantages. One can threaten to kill many more people than it would be profitable to kill. The threat of force follows its own laws. It is effective only to the degree of its credibility. The potential victim is likely to attend to the threat insofar as he believes that his delict will be discovered, that the ruler enjoys the ability to use force, and he will, in fact, attempt to use it. A policeman's life is not a happy one precisely because of mankind's perennial optimistic belief in the improbability of detection, the failure of power, or the failure of nerve. The threat of force, if it is to be successful, must similarly be used judiciously. Overzealous threatening fails to be convincing. Where the most minor crimes receive the death penalty, a man would as soon be hung for stealing a sheep as for a goat.

Thus, a government's power rests upon the willingness of its citizens to deal with small groups of dissidents. It may well be that the very person who is called upon to quell a disturbance will turn out to be more sympathetic to the dissidents than to their own government. They are restrained, however, from acting in terms of their own sympathies by their belief that their sympathy is not widely shared. It is possible to continue ruling under such conditions for generations by maintaining a state of pluralistic ignorance.

In fact, there is always a good deal of uncertainty in regard to the loyalty of subjects. The threat of force, upon which the government rests, disposes most of its citizens to conceal the extent of their dissatisfaction and, ordinarily, to underestimate the extent of dissatisfaction felt by other citizens. Successful revolutions are usually something of a surprise. In retrospect, the weaknesses of the deposed government appear so glaring as to make it difficult to believe that they were not apparent at the time. History always seems more deterministic than current events.

Although pluralistic ignorance is usually used as descriptive of only totalitarian governments, the fact remains that citizens in a democracy are similarly confined to guessing the opinion of their fellow citizens. The 1948 elections in the United States will serve to illustrate the degree to which even the most sophisticated social science techniques fall short of correctly assessing the temper of citizens. Ordinarily, guesses as to the probable choices of citizens at points of crises are highly subject to a bandwagon effect. To the extent that a government is successful in promoting the opinion that citizens will invariably rally to its standard, the reality will continue to mirror the description.

While the threat of force is necessary to keep in check the proclivities to power of the more unruly citizens, most human beings see their obedience to the powers that be as a voluntary submission to duty rather than an involuntary submission to necessity. Rulers normally enjoy the privilege of legitimacy. Contenders for power wisely vie for legitimation. Discussions of legitimation tend to bog down in specifics. In various times and climes, legitimation was assured by representing the mandate of heaven, having the right blood lines, representing substantively or procedurally the will of the people, or, more simply, promising to provide law and order. What makes for acceptance of legitimacy in the mind of an average citizen tends to be the result of the historical accident of the prevailing ideology. Where ideologies conflict, the ultimate dependence of power on force is more obvious.

The power theory is at its best in the study of nations. While power relationships can be studied in families, small groups, clubs, businesses, and mobs, the theory must become more complicated. In all of these areas an appeal to the power of the State is possible. Such being the case, a power imbalance exists only by the leave of the State. Modern States tend to recognize imbalances only for the most limited purposes. Where the Roman paterfamilias was assumed to have the same power over his family that the Emperor enjoyed over his subjects, modern States are quick to intervene where citizens use their power beyond the sphere allotted to them. State regulation of power often extends to the minutest detail. In many cases it is designed deliberately to remove all power imbalances. In such situations even a two-level theory of power will fail to account for the behavior of participants.

Thus, the power theory, when used to analyze cases other than the State, is subject to the same limitations as economic theory. This is, of course, no coincidence. Any general theory must cope with the fact that nations set the rules of the game for their citizens. Any theory that fails to acknowledge this situation fails to describe the data adequately.

Power theory assumes the inequality of power between any two people. As we have seen, it does not cope with situations in which State action has generated a functional equality. Still more seriously, power theory leaves no place for bargaining. The relationship between two people is either one of dominance and obedience or one of war. A disobedient subject is automatically within the Hobbesian relationship of the war of everyman against everyman. Nations are always in this relationship with each other.

In fact, a good deal of bargaining goes on, the participants blithely oblivious to the lack of theoretical foundation for their actions. Power theory, like economic theory, has supplied no rules for bargaining between unequals.

Although both power theory and economic theory are subject to limitations, their limitations are complementary. Power theory assumes inevitable inequality; economic theory assumes inevitable equality. Power theory rests on the essentially involuntary nature of interpersonal relationships; economic theory rests on the essentially voluntary nature of such relationships. Power theory envisions the complete absence of bargaining; economic theory, its ubiquity. Within a larger perspective, actions in the world take place in a mixed mode, compounded partly of elements of power, partly of elements of economic bargaining. Both theories describe limiting cases rarely, if ever, found in practice. It is possible to describe the same situation through the lenses of each of the theories. The analyses will not fit together. We are left, like Dicken's reporter, trying to write an article on Chinese metaphysics by putting together what the encyclopedia says about China with what the encyclopedia says about metaphysics.

What seems to be called for is a "theory of coercive bargaining" to describe situations in the middle of the continuum. The theory will need to borrow from both economic and power theory, but will have to do more than simply mix elements from the two theories. It will have to sketch out some model for bargaining between unequals. It will have to try to determine at what point a participant ceases to depend on the self-interest of the other participants and falls back on the threat of force. This, of course, need not be a single moment. A participant may go through a series of graded appeals, each one containing a less conspicuous argument to economic interest and a more obvious threat to the recourse of force. Such mixed appeals are the stock in trade of a professional negotiator. His skill consists precisely in his ability to select the most judicious combination of carrot and stick. In all probability, negotiation will always remain a fine art. Nevertheless, it is possible to articulate some of the laws that govern the points at which bargains are struck.

The utility of a theory of coercive bargaining is particularly obvious in a discussion of the fulfillment of contracts. In standard economic theory, contracts are always fulfilled. In power theory, contracts are fulfilled only insofar as it is to the interest of the partner to fulfill them.[4] Obviously, in such a situation, the value of a contract is negligible.

In the real world contracts are fulfilled sometimes and partly. Court dockets testify to the frequency of breach of contract. Common notoriety evidences the frequency of renegotiation. These, however, represent only the extreme, formal cases. Like everything else in the world, the clauses of contracts are subject to different constructions by the various partners to the actions. It should come as no great surprise that most participants favor the construction that accords with their own interest. While many of these differences of interpretation are settled by mutual, if not always amicable, discussions, probably still more are resolved through tacit complicity. In a sense contracts, even after they are signed, remain in a state of perpetual negotiation.

What is called for is some concept of elasticity of contract. This might be defined precisely as the proportion of the total commitment that a partner can, with impunity, ignore. More loosely defined, it is the amount you can get away with. Many a successful business exists on the margin allowed by a nice calculation of elasticity. It is only where elasticity is insufficient that matters are brought to the stage of renegotiation or breach of contract.

The calculation of when a contract is likely to be breached is similarly beyond the scope of either economic or power theory. Although contracts are no longer considered sancrosanct, neither is too overt a violation of contracts lightly entertained. Prudent self-interest dictates a consideration of alternate contracts available with other partners and a calculation of the probability of successfully negotiating a satisfactory substitute contract. Even where preferable alternate contracts are readily available, the contract is not always breached. One's ability to negotiate subsequent contracts may be affected by the facility with which one may be known to terminate contracts that turn out to be less propitious than anticipated. The importance of this form of credibility varies widely from industry to industry. Within the newer and more rapidly expanding industries, Barnum's principle often reigns. Where clients abound, the dissatisfaction of previous clients may present no problem. In such areas, it is foolhardy to maintain that honesty is invariably the best policy. To the maxim that breach of contract is bound to catch up with one in the long run, one may cite Keynes' dictum that in the long run we are all dead. Industries, however, change in their level of tolerance of elasticity and breach of contract. Witness the effect of Quaker merchants on retailing.

It is, perhaps, easier to cite the elements that go into calculations of coercive bargaining than to formulate a general theory. Thus, specific discussions of situations tend to describe what I have here called coercive bargaining in a rather realistic fashion. Discussions such as Machlup's analysis of polypoly and polysony,[5] Whyte's discussion of collective bargaining,[6] and Klee's study of surrender [7] include numerous *ad hoc* explanations foreign to both economic and power theory. To the best of my knowledge no one has attempted to sketch out a general series of assumptions for coercive bargaining.

It would be presumptuous of me to assume that I have laid down the guidelines for so ambitious an endeavor. The success or failure of the particular set of assumptions that I will try to articulate should not affect the obvious necessity for the social sciences to come up with theories in this realm. Formulations that fail to meet the criteria cited above will fail similarly to describe adequately the complexities of human interaction.

2

Theory of Coercive Bargaining

The theory of coercive bargaining assumes that in the ordinary course of events two potential partners to a bargain will be unequal in power. Were their relationship to be solely within the realm of power, no bargaining at all would be possible. Several considerations, however, tend to restrict the use of power.

From the point of view of the stronger partner, as we have seen from power theory, the indiscriminate use of power is inefficient. Force tends to destroy the persons from whom we expect to benefit. Injudicious use of the threat of force undermines its credibility and menaces legitimacy. The rational handling of power calls for its minimum use consistent with the attainment of one's goals. The theory of coercive bargaining assumes that people have economic goals in addition to the desire to maximize their own power. Since both of these are likely to be served by the minimum feasible use of power, the strategy can be conceptualized as normally following this line.

The weaker partner will be even more highly motivated to avoid the use of power. Since he is likely to lose a power struggle if negotiations break down, he is normally well disposed to accede to what he considers reasonable demands.

Bargaining under such circumstances assumes the existence of two conditions. First, the partners are willing to consider the at least partial alleviation of a state of war between them. Second, the partners are at least minimally rational. Like both economic theory and power theory, the theory of coercive bargaining assumes rationality.

Since both partners are rationally committed to the minimum use of power consonant with self-interest, the stage is set for negotiation. At what point will the bargain be struck? This question is equivalent to asking, in more economic terms, what the price is. The calculation for determining the point is somewhat more complex than that called for in economic theory. We may take, as a starting point, the price that would be predicted between two equal partners. This is determined by the law of supply and demand in accordance with the classical formulations of the economist. In a bargain between unequal partners, the point will be skewed to favor the stronger partner. The degree of skewness can be considered a linear function of the extent of disparity between the power positions of the partners.

If we assume that both partners are aware of the actual power positions, their concept of a reasonable bargain will be affected. The range of acceptable bargain of the stronger party will be reduced in accordance with the disparity. The weaker party's range will be correspondingly expanded. Under these conditions, it is no more difficult to consummate a bargain between unequals than between equals.

Initial offers on both sides will be couched completely in terms of self-interest, in accordance with the strategy of the minimal use of power described above. If the areas of acceptable bargain for the two partners overlap, a bargain will be concluded completely in terms of self-interest.

It should not be assumed from the absence of reference to the power dimension during the actual negotiations that this dimension has not influenced the course of the bargain. It is the mutual understanding of the positions of the partners along this dimension that has dictated the degree of deviation from the strictly economic price. Only where the two partners are functionally equivalent in power will the negotiation come to resemble the economic model.

If the ranges of an acceptable bargain for the two partners do not overlap, further offers will take the form of escalations in the power dimension. In accordance with the law of minimum use of power, the stronger party's second offer will be based on a mixture of the appeal to self-interest with the least possible threat of force he sees as likely to convince the weaker partner. This may be combined with an expansion of his area of acceptable bargain.

The weaker party's response will take one of three alternative forms: First, he may accept the offer or indicate a corresponding expansion of his range of acceptable bargaining to signal his continued interest. Second, he may stand pat on his previous offer. Third, he may venture a similar escalation in the power dimension. Since the weaker party is normally more highly motivated to avoid the power dimension, the last response is to be expected only in unusual circumstances. It may be expected where the weaker party is ideologically committed to prefer defeat to surrender. Of course, this is an irrational position, although it produces rational benefits. The third alternative of escalation on the part of the weaker party is also likely in situations of uncertainty about the relative power positions of the partners. This is the kind of a situation to which Coser sees conflict as a solution.[1] The theory of coercive bargaining would see conflict as a solution only where the process of negotiation did not succeed in dispelling the uncertainty.

One of the major functions of negotiation is this process of dispelling uncertainty. The two bargainers, during the first round of negotiations, are likely to have only the most imprecise notion of each other's power. As the bargaining proceeds to threats of force, the parties involved must present some information in respect to the sources of their strength in order to make these threats credible. Although the information presented cannot necessarily be presumed to be an unvarnished description of strength, much real information is transmitted. One cannot, after all, expect one's partner to back down just on one's say-so. The process of negotiation is thus, in part, a teaching situation.

It is not only the extent of physical force that is successively revealed in negotiation. As we have seen from the theory of power, force is effective only to the degree that there is a willingness to make use of it. Negotiators use offers and counter-offers as an opportunity to demonstrate to the opposing party their willingness to resort to force should such a recourse be necessary to achieve their goals. As more information becomes available, more realistic settings of the range of acceptable bargain become possible.

Successive stages of negotiation follow the same pattern as the first stage. In time, the parties expand their ranges of acceptable bargain to the point where the negotiation can be concluded or they reveal their unwillingness to make such an expansion. The breakdown of negotiations results in conflict only where the stronger party can find no acceptable substitute partner.

The length of the negotiation is likely to depend upon the amount of uncertainty with which the bargaining process begins as well as the skill of the negotiators and their interest in the bargain, on the one hand, and their intransigence on the other. The length of the negotiation bears no relation to the point at which the negotiation is concluded.

In spite of the numerous opportunities for bluff inherent in the negotiating process, the result is by no means comparable to a poker game. While occasional bluffs are successful, by and large the results of the bargaining process tend to resemble what would be predicted under the initial power positions and economic advantages enjoyed by the partners.

Despite occasionally widespread disparities in the power positions of the partners, negotiation is almost invariably advantageous. As Klee points out, an enemy, no matter how thoroughly defeated, is always left with some advantage with which to bargain. This, let me repeat, assumes the rationality of the persons involved. Of course, there are situations in which negotiations will not take place, for example, the punishment of disobedient subjects. Even here, however, negotiation is not unheard of.

The model of coercive bargaining that I have sketched out works fairly well for negotiation between States and for the negotiation between a State and one or more of its citizens. Given the large disparity between the power of the State and the power of the individual, negotiations of the latter sort tend to resemble Klee's picture of the negotiation of surrender.

In the vast majority of bargains negotiated, the State is not one of the contracting parties. Nevertheless, the bargain cannot be properly understood without taking into account the role of the State. To illustrate, let us consider the model of a perfect marketplace developed by Adam Smith. This model assumes that none of the participants is strong enough to have any individual effect on the price level. If we were to start with such a marketplace, it would probably be a question of time before some individual bargainer or group of bargainers became influential enough seriously to affect price level. Smith's awareness of the motivation of bargainers to such action is evidenced in his statement, "People of the same trade seldom meet together, even for merriment and diversion, but the conversation ends in a conspiracy against the public, or in some contrivance to raise prices." [2]

The preservation of the perfect marketplace requires, then, the determination of the State to break up conspiracies in restraint of trade. This does not require that the State directly intervene in every bargain, although occasional intervention is necessary. It does mean that the State make clear its intention to intervene whenever the perfect marketplace is seriously menaced. We may consider the State as employing a strategy, in game theory terms. In other words, the State articulates in advance what it intends to do in specific circumstances. Given the bargainers' knowledge of the State's strategy, they can, by avoiding the circumstances which provoke intervention, avoid intervention.

The State, of course, need not share Adam Smith's preference for the perfect marketplace. By refusing to commit itself to a strategy aimed at the preservation of competition or by refusing to implement a strategy of preservation, it can allow a monopoly situation to develop. Many States have adopted such a course, finding it much easier to deal with a handful of organized firms than with an army of individual traders. Although the State can adopt, or refuse to adopt, any particular strategy, it cannot fail to affect the state of the marketplace, since the absence of any commitment is also a strategy.

Thus far we have considered the marketplace only in terms of a single dimension: the number and influence of the bargainers involved. The marketplace may be studied in terms of an infinite number of other dimensions. For each of these, the strategy of the State as it is actually implemented is similarly influential.

The change in the nature of the economic marketplace in regard to collective bargaining may be taken as a case in point. The market, as envisioned by the classical economists and the statesmen who attempted to implement their theory, saw workers' associations as conspiracies in restraint of trade, no different from any other monopolistic attempt to dominate the market. The government was committed to the strategy of breaking up such associations and punishing their leaders. Notwithstanding this declared strategy, workers continued to organize. They terminated their employment jointly, a practice which could conceivably be defended in classical economic terms.

It was, however, soon apparent that merely striking was totally inadequate as a weapon, even in the absence of governmental punishment. Being replaced by another worker was not conducive to the prospects of renegotiating a more favorable contract. The process of collective bargaining rapidly escalated into the use of force. The workers forcibly prevented the entrance of alternative contracted parties into the plant or took subsequent punitive measures to discourage the participation of new parties to the contract. Where management felt sufficiently confident of its own power to meet this bargaining position with counterforce, it did so. Where its own threat of force lacked credibility, management's only alternative threat was invoking governmental intervention. Generally, this intervention, despite the official commitment of governmental agencies, failed to materialize, appeared after the damage was done, or turned out, in the long run, to be favorable to the workers. The general regularity of the governmental failure of nerve in implementing its commitments took several decades to become clear. Nevertheless, as workers enjoyed increasingly more confidence that the threat of solicitation of intervention would fail to prove effective, revision of the ranges of acceptable bargain took place. As the willingness of the workers to resort to force and the unwillingness of management and government similarly to resort became established, negotiations were increasingly able to be settled without the ultimate escalation taking place. As collective bargaining agreements were negotiated without the aid of government intervention, the government's official strategy of intervention was changed to recognize the *fait accompli.*

Of course, simultaneous with these negotiations, workers' groups had been pressing governmental agents to make just such a shift in their strategy of commitment. Their success was not unrelated to their voting power, always a consideration in democratically organized governments.

In any event, the present government strategy of nonintervention in defense of the entrance of new parties into the negotiation governs the rules of the marketplace in regard to collective bargaining. Force, on the part of the workers, being tacitly acknowledged as legitimate, its threat is ordinarily sufficient to accomplish the desired end.

Although the resulting marketplace is a far cry from that envisioned by the classical economists, it is, in fact, quite regular, predictable, and viable. It is not necessarily the form that the marketplace will take some decades hence. It may be assumed, however, that changes in the guiding principles of the marketplace will be accompanied by changes in governmental implementation of its strategic commitments. Such changes are normally accompanied by a period of turbulence in which a considerably higher proportion than usual of negotiations are pursued to advanced levels of escalation. As the change is recognized, negotiations once more tend to be settled in earlier rounds.

In summary, the marketplace is an area whose nature is governed by the strategies to which the State has committed itself. It is the State's commitment to action that lays the ground rules under which the marketplace functions. The various laws that Smith articulated to explain the way in which the marketplace operates are not natural laws corresponding to the law of the rate of falling bodies in physics. They are expectations about how the marketplace will behave in the situation of a given set of governmental strategy. Even a slight shift in the State's commitments can change the rules of the game substantially.

While Smith's interest is limited to the economic marketplace, modern States have a large number of areas that operate in similar fashion. The State commits itself to act in certain circumstances. In the absence of such circumstances, the area is permitted to go its own way, following its own rules. Thus, family life, clubs, educational enterprises, religious societies, and a host of other groups pursue their own interactions, subject to the limitations imposed by the State's commitment to intervene. In all of these the State's strategy, even where it does not lead to intervention, sets up the rules by which interaction is governed.

We may call such areas enclaves. We will define enclaves as semiautonomous quasi-societies. Despite Adam Smith's characterization of the marketplace as free, it is clear that its freedom is rather fragile, being subject to the State's maintenance of the appropriate strategy. The best that the marketplace can hope for is a semiautonomous state, in which it can develop itself, subject to the perennial limitation imposed by the possibility of State action. The areas in question preempt only a single aspect of the individual's life. However devoted the economic man may be to the accumulation of property, his economic activities represent only part of his life. His interactions, in the marketplace as well as out of it, include other aspects of human interrelationship. While he may, if he so choose, neither marry nor pray nor educate himself, yet he cannot prevent himself from being seen as a target by willing brides, missionaries, and educational administrators. Associations within the various enclaves are often nothing loath to spread their activities into other areas of human life. Business and professional groups hold conventions; churches play the stock market; husband-hunting young women go to school; and educational institutions do research. What keeps in check these expansionist proclivities is not the absence of motivation on the part of the participants, but the jaundiced eye with which the State views societies with such totalitarian tendencies. An association that begins to preempt the whole of a citizen's life is rightly understood to be a menace to the State. Such associations fare very poorly in modern society. They are subject to constant harassment. Eventually, they must either limit their objectives or take over the State.

It is now the conventional practice in political science to explain the rise of totalitarian governments in just such a fashion as the takeover of a government by a political party.[3] The political parties in question almost invariably turn out to have been distinctive not only for their encompassing ideology but for their development of associated youth groups, sport clubs, and other branches not conventionally expected of a political party. The extent of their members' time devoted to party activities was usually far in excess of that normally included within a single enclave. The preemptive nature of party membership continues even after the takeover. It is one of the most commonly remarked characteristics of totalitarian governments. For our purposes, the question of whether the government has absorbed the party or vice versa is not particularly relevant.

We may see the State, then, as spinning off a large number of enclaves. These enclaves are governed by the strategy of the State. The State, moreover, maintains a perpetual, if sporadic, vigilance that the strategy it has adopted is producing the desired results, as well as that the promised forthcoming intervention is actually taking place.

Although we speak of State power as prior to the regularities of the enclave, it must be borne in mind that this is a logical priority rather than a temporal one. Unquestionably, enclaves such as family life or the sexual marketplace have antedated the rise of government by millennia. The terminology rests on the assumption that it is governmental strategy that dictates the nature of the enclaves and not vice versa. In any particular case, the government may decide to adapt its strategy to the conditions developing in the enclave. It retains, nonetheless, the inevitable option of modifying the enclave to suit its own desires.

The logical relationship is often obscured by an ideological commitment to maintain that one's actions are nothing more than a response to the demands of the situation. Where such ideology is widespread, it becomes possible to interpret the result in some term such as Reisman's notion of the veto power of citizens' groups.

Historically, not all societies have spun off such enclaves. The areas of life within a primitive tribe are so tightly interrelated that it is scarcely fruitful to attempt to understand their sociology in terms of enclaves. Similarly, within well-organized, highly developed totalitarian States, the control of all areas of life is so tightly organized and the intervention so direct and arbitrary that enclaves can scarcely be said to exist.

Other societies have lacked enclaves for opposing reasons. Either they have been so disorganized that governmental authority has not been able to establish the strategic control that enclaves require or they have been the scene of conflicting ideologies. In these cases the areas of society which would otherwise be enclaves achieve autonomy. The most conspicuous example of this situation was medieval Christendom where the rivalry between the Church and State left all men citizens of two worlds.

The central government cum enclaves can readily be seen as one of the solutions on the centralization-decentralization continuum. That this solution has been embraced by the overwhelming proponderance of modern societies argues for its inevitability given the nature of the twentieth century's technology of force and dominant ideologies. There is no particular reason to expect that the twenty-third century will see a similar combination. In any event, I will leave it to others to investigate the necessary conditions for the development of the central government cum enclaves solution and return to my consideration of the implications that this solution has for coercive bargaining.

Although describing the State's commitment to intervention as a strategy serves as a convenient heuristic device for explaining its effect on enclaves, the situation in real life is nowise so clear-cut. The bulk of the State's commitments are articulated in writing at tedious length. Any particular word in this voluminous literature is subject to interpretation and other forms of misunderstanding. Despite the Anglo-Saxon presumption that all men understand the law, lawyers enjoy the most widespread doubts. In fact, one of the modern schools of jurisprudence defines the law as the best guess as to what the judge will decide. In the event, the skills of the contending attorneys as well as the particular prejudices of the judge may sizably affect the verdict. Thus, though the rules of an enclave are laid down by what a government says it will do, the nature and extent of its commitment is a question of probability rather than certainty. A large proportion of bargains are concluded in the vast gray area where the government's intentions are doubtful, the subject of anxious hope and not calm foreknowledge.

The situation is complicated still further by the fact that numerous bureaus in the government are ever at work extending, revising, and nullifying the government's commitments. Where, to the best of one's knowledge, the government is committed to the support of the other party to the bargain, there is still room for hope that a change in policy will swing the balance to one's favor. Since, as Aubrey Menen points out, it is as hard to stop making rules as it is to stop eating almonds,[4] this hope is by no means illusory. The volume of commitments grows apace. It is presently beyond the ability of even the most expert to master more than a limited segment of the literature. Parties to complex bargains frequently hire an expert or a staff of experts in the hope of arriving at a better guess as to the government's commitments. Still more significantly, larger scale enterprises often hire personnel whose task is primarily to argue for changes in the government's pattern of commitments. The continued employment of such persons suggests that they manage to meet with some degree of success.

Even where the government's commitment is reasonably clear it may not be easy to predict whether a specific intervention will be forthcoming. The State of New York, for example, has had on the books for over a decade a law that commits it to punish severely State employees who go out on strike. Although violators can be detected with no more than perusal of the front pages of the daily newspapers, the promised intervention has never taken place. Neither can bargainers be assured that intervention in the absence of commitment or even in violation of other commitments will not occur. John Kennedy, then President of the United States, in response to a rise in steel prices, ordered government agencies to refuse to accept bids from U.S. Steel, despite the illegality of this action. In spite of the solidity of its case, and its possession of ample resources, U.S. Steel chose to lower its prices rather than hazard its fortune in the courts.

Whether an intervention will or will not occur is, except in the most extreme cases, difficult to predict. Whether the results of such intervention turn out in your favor or in the favor of the other party can be seen with assurance only in retrospect. In the ordinary course of events, negotiators are understandably loath to provoke an intervention so likely to be of dubious benefit.

Of course, the extent and nature of intervention is affected by the prevailing climate of ideology. When Andrew Johnson removed the money of the United States from the National Bank, an action clearly within the scope of Federal power, the uproar was several orders of magnitude louder than the apathetic reaction generated by Kennedy's action, cited above. Bargainers who feel that their own self-interest is seen by the community as worthy of governmental beneficence are likely to be considerably more sanguine about the prospects that intervention will turn out well. Since government officials normally enjoy a latitude of action far in excess of the putative rigidity of State commitments, opportunities for more idiosyncratic favoritism are not hard to come by. Collusion is not unheard of.

What then will bargaining look like under these circumstances? Obviously the model that I have sketched out will be inadequate to the complexities involved. Partners to a bargain will take into account not only their economic interest and their relative power positions but also the probability, nature, and extent of governmental intervention. Insofar as the parties, to the best of their knowledge, anticipate the possibility that the government will intervene, the relative power that they would enjoy in the absence of such intervention is changed. The point of the bargain is skewed a second time in the direction of the favored party. The extent of second-order skewness is a linear function of the disparity of favor enjoyed under governmental commitments. Since, however, the promised intervention is a probability rather than a certainty, the extent of this skewness must be multiplied by the probability of intervention. All of the figures involved are likely to be guesses. Nevertheless, game theory demonstrates that sophisticated calculations can be made even under these limitations.

The range of an acceptable bargain previously calculated as the range of economic advantage, expanded or contracted in accordance with the disparity of power to the disadvantage or advantage, respectively, of the particular party, must now be recalculated with the expansion or contraction a function of the party's power advantage given the probability of State intervention. Once the parties have made this calculation, the bargaining may go on somewhat as before. The modification in power position that results from possible influence of the State differs from other power advantages only in respect to its greater uncertainty. Since, time out of mind, both business ventures and power plays have had their element of risk, the intrinsic nature of the game is not changed substantially.

Just as the possibility of escalation affects the point at which a bargain is struck, even if the possible escalation never takes place, the available alternative of escalation into the solicitation of intervention has far more widespread effects than the comparative rarity of such solicitation would suggest. The party anticipating benefits from intervention contracts his range of acceptable bargain in accordance with the probability and extent of such benefits. To the extent that the nature of governmental intervention is unclear, its possibility tends to protract the bargaining process. Bargainers tend to overestimate the probable benefits to be achieved from intervention. Since bargainers are likely to be optimistic in temperament, it is not unusual for both parties to a bargain to contract the range of acceptable bargain in anticipation of the favor of the government. Thus, the overlap in range which is necessary if a bargain is to be struck, may diminish in size or disappear completely. To the degree that bargainers are willing, as the discussion proceeds, to waive the chimeric possibilities of intervention benefits in favor of the immediate advantages of concluding a bargain, negotiations can be terminated without either party resorting to the solicitation of intervention.

We may assume that the strategy of the minimum use of power will apply with equal force to the power to be derived from the successful manipulation of government intervention, or its threat. Given the inherent uncertainty involved in government intervention, this form of power is ordinarily the most dangerous form available to a negotiator. Under normal circumstances, the hierarchy of escalation goes from the threat of force to force to the threat of solicitation of intervention to solicitation.

As before, both parties begin with an appeal to economic interest. Where the offers reveal that their ranges of acceptable bargain do not overlap, the stronger party makes a second offer based on economic interest combined with the minimum threat of force he sees as likely to provoke acceptance of his terms. The weaker party now enjoys a more extensive range of alternatives than under the previous model. He may accept, stand pat, counter with a threat of force, or, should he feel that his own threat of force is unconvincing, counter with the threat of appeal to intervention. Given the increased uncertainty that the possibility of intervention brings, one of the last two responses becomes more probable.

We thus find that possibility of government intervention produces paradoxical results. While it makes negotiation possible, it tends to complicate the negotiation and to make it more likely that the course of negotiation will be dictated by the power position of the participants rather than their economic advantage. This limitation appears inherent in the government's desire to affect the terms of the negotiation.

3

The Educational Enclave

The present chapter attempts to demonstrate that education constitutes an enclave, as it has been defined in the previous chapter, and that the interrelationships in the educational enclave can fruitfully be considered in terms of bargain and contract. Once this has been done, we can devote our efforts to exploration of the characteristic features of the educational bargain.

There is little problem in establishing the right of education to be considered a quasi-society. Even though most of those participating in education are formally supposed to be devoting all of their time to this endeavor, a cursory glance at scheduling should serve to dispel this illusion. If we may rely on Rickover's data, about one half of the days of the year are devoted to education in Europe; in the United States the proportion is considerably lower. Even on days presumably dedicated to education, the number of hours spent fall far short of even present-day lax standards of working hours. Nor can all the time spent under officially supervised educational activities legitimately be considered preemptive of their participants' occupation with other aspects of life. It would be belaboring the point to insist, further, that even the most dedicated of educational participants manages to retain some degree of noneducational life. There seems no danger of confusing education with what Goffman calls a total institution.

The question of the extent of autonomy of the educational area is somewhat more ticklish. Given the power of the State in modern societies, we need not be overly concerned with the theoretical possibility that education has managed to attain complete autonomy. The complementary possibility that the autonomy of the educational area has been so far vitiated that its claims to enclave status are no longer valid can be disposed of only with some difficulty. Some one hundred and fifty years ago there would have been no question of the description of education as an enclave. All States recognized education as a private enterprise, left to the initiative of associations of interested citizens or individual entrepreneurs. Adam Smith discusses the wages and living conditions of professors in much the same spirit as he deals with other hired help. If the State took any interest in the field, it was as likely to be preoccupied with the danger that the lower classes would be taught too much for their own good as to be concerned with the other inadequacies of education. The rise of democratic governments altered this picture considerably.

The educational area can be roughly divided into four levels: the primary, the secondary, the college, and the graduate. These are normally participated in sequentially. At the present time more than half of the educational endeavors on the first two levels are directly run by the State and the remaining endeavors on these levels are rather directly and closely supervised. I will make some passing mention of primary and secondary education later on in the book as analogous to the results to be expected from extrapolation of certain tendencies in the educational enclave. In present-day society primary and secondary education must be considered as falling within the pale of direct State activities. The educational enclave is limited to college and graduate levels. Even on these levels the government often maintains educational institutions. The pattern of interaction, however, is for the moment still governed indirectly through the strategy of intervention.

Now to the consideration of the utility of understanding educational relationships as a series of transactions, that is, negotiations, bargains, and contracts. It is of the essence of a bargain that it involve the exchange of economic goods.

The consideration of education as a transaction raises some problems immediately. It is at first obvious that payment is made by the student in several forms, only one of which is money. In some cases, no money at all changes hands. Evaluation of the product that the educational institution proposes to give in return for this mixed bag presents further problems. How then is such a heterodox exchange to be compared to the elegant paradigm of classical economics?

In order to do so, we will have to reconsider the basic assumptions of economics. This is an extreme course, granted, but then I am not myself an economist.

Classical economics took as its ideal type of exchange a small transaction by a small shopkeeper, such as the proprietor of a grocery selling a quart of milk to a customer. Here, the customer pays in cash for a tangible item. The vendor has himself purchased this item. He must sell, over the long run, at a price that covers the cost of the item, the item's share in the fixed costs of the business, the labor involved in one fashion or another in the transaction, and, hopefully, a degree of profit. Thus far the system works exceedingly well.

Let us suppose, however, that our good grocer, after a sufficient number of years of illustrating Mr. Smith's maxims, decides to sell his business. He possesses various items of his stock in trade still awaiting purchasers; he has, perhaps, a building and fixtures. The value of all of these he can assess with a tolerable degree of exactitude. In addition, he will demand from the new grocer a sum for good will. In return, he will give some guarantee that he will not open a competitive store in the neighborhood for a fixed period of time. The new grocer, oblivious to the problems he presents to Mr. Smith, agrees. What is the nature of the good will being sold? And, from whence does it come? Veblen, with his eye on the machinations of captains of industry, considers it a device of the businessman to line his own purse at the expense of others. But our humble grocer emeritus seems highly unlikely to have stumbled, after so many years of impeccable business behavior, into the role of confidence man. He is sure he is selling a real, if intangible, asset. And who are we to say that our new grocer is acting irrationally? It would seem that he is buying, along with the fixtures, an amount of prestige.

But how has our retiring grocer accumulated this prestige? He did not have it in the palmy days when he first opened his shop. We are forced to conclude that he must have gotten it from his customers, along with the shillings and pence they gave for his products. Certainly, we can say that, *ceteris paribus,* the larger the number and size of the transactions, the greater the prestige he has accrued. Classical economics is able to get along without mention of this secondary transaction by considering the grocer as taking part in a virtually infinite number of transactions. As a result, the amount of prestige given in each transaction will be negligible. Therefore, disregarding the prestige allows an approximate description of the transaction which is not too far from the actual case. It is only when we look at the grocer retiring after years of transactions that we detect an unaccounted-for asset.

The problem may be illuminated by another example. Suppose we have two tailors. One serves one thousand customers regularly. The other serves 999 customers and the president of the United States. From the point of view of classical economics, these worthy tradesmen are in parallel circumstances. Yet a prospective buyer of these concerns would in all rationality expect to pay appreciably more for the latter situation. Furthermore, if our fortunate tailor decided to give the president a more reasonable rate than he charged his other customers in order to maintain his patronage, we would not presume that this was an irrational act. We are then forced to conclude again that the customer has been giving prestige as part of the transaction. Thus far, we have considered situations in which the buyer has conferred prestige on the seller. But we cannot assume that the action is unidirectional. James Duesenberry [1] considers a series of somewhat different transactions. To give an example, one which Mr. Duesenberry does not cite, the possession in 1948 of a television set conferred, in addition to the privilege of watching mechanized shadows on the cave wall, an intangible asset, which we may consider prestige. There is, then, a class of transactions where the buyer acquires both product and prestige. While Mr. Duesenberry examines at length the effect that differential amounts of prestige have on pricing and marketing policies, it is not necessary at this point to follow into the intricacies of his argument. Suffice it to say he is forced to postulate a drive to higher consumption based on the effect on self-esteem of an increase in social status, a significant departure from the basic picture of a transaction developed by classical economics, in order to explain levels of prices and savings.

We can see, then, that the classical explanation is a limiting case, even as an economic transaction. In all transactions, we may find that, in association with the exchange of purchase price and product, there takes place an exchange of prestige. In varying circumstances, the prestige exchange is more or less important compared with the tangible exchange. While it is never entirely absent, its effect may be so small as to be considered negligible. This is the case that has been taken by the classical economists as the typical example, although it is in fact quite unusual.

As has been adumbrated above, the classical economists have been able to do this only by considering businesses that cater to a large number of customers. The explanation would fall short of describing, for example, the activities of a market research company. Here, the number of clients is relatively small. An enterprising market research company is quite aware of the prestige advantage of having a client whose name is well known. As a rule, research companies are asked, when they are soliciting business, for whom they have done work in the past. A client with a famous name will be treated with a deference unlikely to be accorded to a less well-known competitor. The ubiquity of the question suggests that clients are equally sensitive to the prestige advantages of using a well-known research agency. Although the degree to which considerations of prestige are the deciding factor in the consummation of a transaction in this field cannot be readily ascertained, common notoriety would indicate that their effort is not negligible.

If the foregoing analysis is to be adopted, it would seem necessary to construct a calculus of prestige to supplement the calculus of costs with which the economists have been preoccupied. Such, indeed, is my contention. At first blush, this is a formidable task. Prestige does not come in readily quantifiable units; its consideration is not free of the taint of subjectivity; its very presence is by inference. Yet, if we are to go along with Little's astringent account of welfare economics, much analysis is based on the concept of happiness, a state of mind ascertained with some difficulty and not easily quantifiable.[2] Nevertheless, economic analysis is not on this basis impossible to make or challengeable when made. The construction of such a calculus of prestige is beyond my capacities. The demonstration of the advantages of such a mathematical treatment is sufficient task for the moment.

The analysis of transactions is, in fact, still more complicated than the above argument suggests. For the exchange of prestige in itself involves costs. Certain expenditures are necessary to acquire the prestige to transfer to others. As we have seen, a tailor might reduce the price of a suit to a well-known person in order to benefit from the prestige of a famous clientele. The difference in price must be considered as an expense involved in the acquisition of prestige, howbeit justified. The customer may make similar sacrifices to acquire the prestige he brings to the transaction. All of these costs in money and effort, neglected in more orthodox analyses, must be considered as prestige costs. Any attempt to integrate prestige costs and gains with the usual economic considerations on a systematic basis is, *a fortiori,* beyond the range of this book.

Fortunately, education is a limiting case. It is possible to consider transactions in education as sufficiently concentrated in the realm of prestige exchange so that the more usual money-product exchange can in most cases be considered negligible. From the point of view of the institution, the production of a diploma is an insignificant cost. Expensive buildings are reared and costly faculties are hired not to manufacture diplomas, but to generate prestige. It is the right to possess the diploma rather than the diploma itself which is the end of the student. A complete disregard of the costs of production of the diploma itself, then, does little violence to a description of the educational transaction from this point of view.

The student, for his part, pays in money, time, effort, and prestige. Of these various expenditures, the time, effort, and prestige are directly oriented toward the augmenting of the prestige of the student or of the institution. The money paid must be considered as falling in both realms. Generally, the greater the sums involved in student fees, the greater the proportion in the realm of prestige cost. In any event this expense is the least of considerations once the transaction has begun. Only to this degree will our consideration of education fall into the usual categories.

Although education represents a rather extreme example of concentration in the prestige area, it is by no means unique in this regard. Reference should be made at this point to situations in other enclaves where similar treatment is indicated.

For example, a research agency with which I was associated used several consultants. These gentlemen were characterized largely by the possession of academic degrees. Their consultantships required no actual expenditure of time, effort, or sagacity, but rested on a transaction by which they gave the agency the right to list their names in reports and proposals in return for their right to style themselves in their own business dealings as consultants to this prestigious organization. No money changed hands. In classical terms, this could hardly have been considered a transaction at all. While the consultants dedicated their time, money, and prestige to earning the degrees that produced the prestige they contributed and the agency was at some equivalent pains to develop the reputation that generated the prestige it contributed, all of this activity bore no fruit in any tangible product. The transaction may be considered an even more clear-cut limiting case than most educational transactions.

It may also be pointed out that the narrow range of the classical paradigm may be accountable for the widespread confusion in interpreting the role of advertising. Given the understanding of transactions in classical terms, it is natural to assume that advertising serves to bring the existence of the vendor to the notice of the buyer. Although this is certainly a secondary effect of advertising, it would seem more reasonable to consider advertising fundamentally as a cost incurred in the manufacture of prestige. In those many items in which the prestige exchange overshadows the money-product exchange, the expenditure of funds on advertising proportionately in excess of the cost of manufacturing the item is no longer the anomaly that it would appear to be in the traditional schema. The engagement of draftsmen for the production of a commercial is, then, no more to be considered irrational than the hiring of a faculty.

One more question remains to be explored before we conclude that our analysis of transactions is tenable. Have we in the course of our argument expanded the notion of transaction beyond its reasonable limits and so subtly perverted the entire concept of transaction? It would not seem so. We have defined an economic transaction as the exchange of economic goods. The exchange of a bundle of motley goods for a similarly variegated collection is not the less an exchange, however more complicated the calculations involved. Situations, therefore, in which the exchange of prestige is combined with a tangible exchange present no problems. But what of the set-up in which the exchange is limited to prestige alone?

First, this extension seems justified on the grounds that prestige is, in fact, an economic good. Prestige can certainly on occasion be converted into cash. It is most evident in the practice of testimonials, where a renowned athlete testifies to his enjoyment of a breakfast food, a smoke, or a razor blade. His approbation must be considered an exercise of prestige rather than an expert opinion. Often the mere appearance of a photograph of a celebrity is considered sufficient to warrant payment, no judgment at all being appended. Cases such as these, however, are belaboring the obvious. It is a fact of the everyday world that amounts of prestige considerably below the amounts required to appear in advertisements are regularly felt to be a significant advantage. Furthermore, a good deal of what can be considered economic, and even at times commercial, effort goes into the acquisition of prestige. While some of this effort can be assumed to be directed toward the acquisition of prestige in and of itself, a little thought will suggest that the accompanying economic benefits generally play no small share in the endeavor.

As we have seen, however, the expenditure of prestige does not necessarily leave the donor poorer in this commodity. This might seem to argue against the inclusion of prestige with economic goods. But it is only in the simplest economic paradigm that each party to the transaction loses what he trades. In an investment, for instance, the investor not only expects to recover his contribution to the bargain, but gain a profit in the bargain. It is true that investments are normally explained in terms of the simpler model by saying that the investor surrenders his ability to make use of the money during the intervening time. Although this may be a dubious economic explanation, let us leave it for the nonce and proceed to look at a still more complicated transaction where explanation in terms of the simple model of mutual loss is not moot, but clearly inadequate.

Suppose I buy something and pay for it with a promissory note, that is, a piece of paper certifying my intention to pay some months hence. What have I lost? The money with which I hopefully intend to pay cannot, at this stage of the bargain, be lost; it does not exist as yet. Nor can I be said to have lost the use of it in the intervening time until it comes into existence. It is precisely this transaction which has given me this use. Nor does the storekeeper with whom I am dealing sacrifice the use. He proceeds to treat my note as currency and, although losing a small discount to cover the possibility that I may renege on my payment, in all other respects is as well off as though I had paid him cash. The result of our mutual transaction is to increase the total amount of currency in circulation.

The transaction is clearly magical. Where before there existed fifty dollars' worth of stock on the storekeeper's shelf and no money in my pocket, I now have fifty dollars' worth of merchandise, and the storekeeper, fifty dollars. Economists find themselves somewhat unsettled by the more supernatural aspects of credit transaction. They try their best to reduce them to simpler models of transaction. Everyone, they say, has a more or less fixed level of credit available to him. His promissory notes draw against this fixed level, lowering it by an amount exactly equal to the size of the promissory note. See, the rabbit was in the hat all the time. Unfortunately, it will not wash.

A while back, I found myself in straitened circumstances. As I attempted to capitalize on the supposedly fixed fund of credit with which the economists tell me I am endowed, I discovered that I had previously made the mistake of buying commodities only when I had the money to pay for them. Since I owed no man any money, I was a poor credit risk. It turns out that people who regularly live beyond their income, so long as they manage in one fashion or another to meet payments as they fall due, are the best credit risks. Notwithstanding the explanations of the economists, every use of credit does not shrink the possibilities of obtaining further credit, but augments them by the extent of the indebtedness. Not only then does my putative spending not diminish my assets, it augments them, if only I know the right way to spend.

Compared to this, the prestige exchanges that we have been discussing are the very model of sobriety.

Moreover, considering prestige as outside the domain of economic goods presents rather more problems than it solves. For example, it has been a recurrent policy for a king whose financial situation is unfavorable to sell patents of nobility. On occasion these have been accompanied by various financial and legal privileges, but this has not been the case invariably. If this is not to be considered a transaction, we are left with the alternative of considering the transfer of money as a gift. But this hardly describes the intent of the parties, or does it meet with the common understanding of the situation. If then we are to consider the event as a transaction, how can we avoid considering an exchange of prestige in a similar vein?

We must then conclude that the inclusion of prestige exchanges in the concept of transactions leaves us with rather more internal consistency than less. Despite the novelty of the approach, we may consider a student's acquisition of an education an economic transaction.

I have, thus far, attempted to argue that prestige exchanges are transactions, without making it a point to distinguish between different kinds of prestige or different transactions that might occur in this realm. I have shown that some transactions include prestige exchanges almost inadvertently and in a sufficiently peripheral fashion to escape the notice of the economists, to say nothing of the persons involved. In other transactions, the effect of prestige is noticeable and, at times, is taken into calculation by the parties to the bargain. In still other transactions, the prestige exchange seems to be the critical consideration, with more conventional elements subsidiary or entirely absent. All of these I have heretofore indifferently denoted prestige exchanges. I now proceed to a more careful examination of the nature of prestige and its origins.

Ultimately, prestige derives from the opinion of the community. Any culture tends to honor certain traits. What these may be will depend on the culture. Some admire heroism, others piety. One culture encourages cunning, another restraint, another creativity. The list could be extended indefinitely. Cultures within the memory of man have extolled productivity. Present culture, according to some theorists, honors sophistication of consumption. For the moment, we may regard the trait itself as irrelevant. We may consider prestige as the recognition accorded by a community to the putative possessors of a specific trait. While it will be necessary later to modify this simplified definition, it is a good starting point for examining the vicissitudes of the awarding process.

Assume that the original trait in any community will fall in a normal curve distribution. There will be a few who possess none of the trait, a few who possess the trait to a marked degree, and many who possess the trait in moderate amounts. The calculable proportion, as well as the basis for the argument, may be found in any standard statistical text.

The trait, then, may be considered as the first order of prestige. All subsequent tokens and recognitions assume the existence of the trait and its differential distribution in the population.

The trait itself is an imaginary construct. Nature, for example, does not contain height. It contains a number of people, some of whom are taller than others. We may conceptualize a dimension, height, which denotes the standard of comparison we are using to rank other people. In the case of height, the evaluation of people is comparatively easy. If we attempt to measure overweight, the operation, even when we can agree on conceptualizing the trait, is appreciably more difficult. The measurement of heroism, self-restraint, or piety is still more knotty. Of necessity, traits difficult to measure will be assessed in a more imprecise fashion.

We have been speaking here of two types of complications. Height and overweight are traits of existence. Although there may be practical difficulties in arriving at a measurement or index of overweight, it is theoretically possible. Given sufficient desire and sophistication of theory, we may expect precise measurements, in time. Heroism, however, is a trait of behavior. Some people have the opportunity to display such a trait, while others with presumably equivalent natural endowments may never have been placed in a situation to evoke it. It is possible to conceive of a laboratory situation which presents all persons with an equal opportunity to rise to a specific occasion. Such a test would, however, at best present an index of heroism rather than a measurement. Heroism is conceived to be a trait that is manifested in a variety of ways in different situations, of which our laboratory test would be only a sample. Moreover, it would still be possible that previous experience in situations calling for heroism would enter the tests as a contaminating factor. In the real world, however, even so limited a degree of precision is unlikely.

By and large, prestige rests on traits of behavior. It is of course possible to accord prestige to tall people, for example. Most prestige, however, is not of this type. Prestige accorded lineage, while the lineage is a trait of existence, rests on the supposed behavior of forebears. Even the possession of wealth is assumed to reflect some abilities of acquisition on the part of either the present possessor or his ancestors.

We may consider a specific behavior or cluster of behaviors as the second order of prestige. Of necessity, the estimation of possession of a trait of behavior will lead to a somewhat different result than what we might arrive at could we estimate the possession directly. This discrepancy is one, however, which is customarily tolerated by the community with ease.

The discrepancy is, in fact, wider than we have pictured. The motivations of men are many and varied. Behavior that we have assigned as indicative of a particular trait will in specific instances be undertaken for quite other reasons. This, too, has been accepted as part of the human condition.

Nor can the alternative motivations that might precipitate the behavior in question be considered random. The veriest toddler will be aware of the behaviors upon which the community dotes. Most men desire the approbation of the community. Many a man considers the community's good opinion of him a prerequisite for a good opinion of himself.[3] Now, while the underlying trait may not be learned,[4] the behaviors presumed to reflect them can be. More persons, then, will demonstrate behavior indicative of a trait than might be expected by pure chance.

This discrepancy is of a magnitude greater than the previous and its existence can scarce escape the notice of the community. It is almost always possible to make a virtue of necessity, however. Prestige will be conceptualized as accorded to those who possess the trait and demonstrate the energy to develop the latent attribute. It is seen as only equity that those who strive to manifest approved behavior despite initial handicaps should be at least equally rewarded with those who are naturally endowed through no effort of their own. Of course, all the striving will come to naught if the claimant does not succeed in demonstrating the behavior, but this is a circumstance which no one will credit to himself.

In a small group of perhaps half a dozen people, the behavior of all is known to all and such marks of respect as are paid to the possessors of any particular trait are likely to be automatic. In a larger community, this cannot be assumed to be the case. There arises a third order of prestige, some token of prestige, which serves to cue the stranger that its bearer is entitled to some quantum of respect. The variety of means of identification of the prestigious is as wide as the imagination of man. Honorific titles, distinctive headdresses or other apparel, tattooing, the right to a retinue, the right to some form of prescribed or proscribed behavior on the right of the unprestiged, all have been and are used. For our purposes, we need not distinguish between tokens, but merely consider the common element: the identification of the prestiged.

With the existence of this third order, a new source of discrepancy between the rolls of the prestiged and the possession of the underlying trait is possible. We now have several sources for the according of prestige, where heretofore we had one. Undoubtedly, the criteria used for evaluating the behavior of candidates vary somewhat, depending on the source of the accreditation. Given the best will in the world—a commodity often postulated but hard come by—there will be some bearers of the token who are less than worthy and individuals with valid claims untokened. In casual conversation, one cannot properly assess another's claim to the possession of a token. One needs must accept the holder as entitled to the prestige.

Although tokens are a convenience to the community, we should not, therefore, attribute their origin to their utility. Man is a symbolic animal and is likely to convert to ritual most anything that comes to hand. Tokens of prestige are found in any community, whether or not there is apparent need. Man is often incapable of appreciating the substance without the symbol.

Be that as it may, the convenience of tokens in identifying persons to whom or occasions at which deference is in order is not without its price. It tends subtly to exploit the phenomena it is intended to mirror. Where at first the purple feather is the privilege of those whom the community delights to honor, in time it is

the feather itself that carries the prestige, and questions of qualification are relegated to the background. All wearers are equal. It
is the uniform, not the man, you salute.

Prestige, by now, has begun to take on a life of its own. Its connection with the trait it is purported to represent has become
considerably qualified. Nor is the end of this process of disen-
gagement in sight. Let us pursue the exploration of the autonomy of prestige a step further.

When a man has received a signal mark of prestige, it is not he
alone who is honored thereby. His relatives take pride in their
kinship with him. His friends are buoyed up. His acquaintances
are less casual. Any who have dealings with him are likely to feel
that some of his prestige has rubbed off on them. And so it has.
The president's tailor, the king's valet, the queen's confection-
naire, all enjoy a real, if derivative, prestige, one which, as we
have seen, is convertible to cash.

We have, then, a fourth order of prestige, prestige by association. The prestige involved is likely to be incidental to the token
holder. It is certainly not entirely under his control. He may
select those with whom he wishes to associate. He can hardly
choose not to associate at all. Moreover, he will usually have
motives other than the spreading of prestige in mind on continuing the association. While the president's association with
local politicians in election years shows his awareness of the
strength of prestige leakage, his association with his tailor is
likely to be decided on other grounds.

The beneficiaries of prestige leakage do not lay claim to the
possession of the underlying trait. The associates of a famous athlete do not derive their importance from being themselves ath-
letic. The mere existence of this fourth order is prima facie evidence the prestige has come to have a meaning of its own which
transcends the trait it is designed to signalize. The prestige for
any particular trait has acquired something of a character which
makes it resemble the prestige of all other traits. It is not entirely
a negotiable currency, but it is possible to convert it with some
discount into other prestiges or other goods.

Upon what can this negotiability of prestige be assumed to

rest? Perhaps our presumption that prestige is intended to be accorded for a single trait is inadequate. We have already seen that it is necessary to broaden the formulation to include a recognition of effort spent to develop the trait. A consideration of the circumstances in which prestige is accorded tends to argue for some greater complexity. For example, à hero receives an award for wiping out an enemy machine-gun nest. Yet if he were to undertake the same risk to save a stray cat, he seems unlikely to be similarly recognized. There would seem to be an element of wisdom being rewarded. Granted this is the wisdom of advancing the interests of the State rather than the wisdom of self-preservation, but this is irrelevant. Similarly, the reward in oratorical contests goes regularly to those who have the sagacity to praise the Constitution rather than the temerity to criticize it. It would seem, then, that prestige is awarded to clusters of traits rather than to a single trait. Likewise, we shall see in our later analysis of the educational system that institutions are dependent on a student body with proper proportions of students with intelligence, prowess at the tournaments, and high status. According to the conventional understanding of education, the presence of these last two groups is irrational. On the other hand, the assumption that the prestige bestowed by education is intended to recognize all of these traits accounts neatly for the dependence.

It is beyond the scope of this volume to examine the basis for according all kinds of prestige. The few examined do suggest that we are warranted in assuming that a token recognizes a cluster of traits with no necessary connection to each other. If this is the case, it may well be that the bestowal of any token assumes that the recipient is the bearer of an admirable character. In fact, many tokens articulate this assumption overtly, much as a commission in the army declares the recipient to be an officer and a gentleman. Even when the assumption is not openly declared it seems to be publicly accepted. All tokens of prestige seem in part a recognition of the recipient's mana.

It is then not surprising that persons who have achieved prestige in one field are often gratuitously credited with competence in all fields. Einstein, for example, was looked to for political advice, although his pronouncements on social questions showed no evidence of mathematical training. Baseball stars, notoriously, have superior judgment on cereals, razors, and juvenile delinquency. There is, in fact, a general expectation that specific prestiges are appropriate for those who have acquired other prestiges.

Prestige leakage is then not so inexplicable a phenomenon as it appeared at first. Those who associate with a person of excellent character cannot be entirely lacking in admirable characteristics of their own. They may be praiseworthy for other traits, but some excellence must be expected of them.

Consideration of the general character of the candidate would seem to make the awarding of tokens considerably more difficult. There is virtually no consensus on what constitutes good character. In practice, it is necessary for awarding bodies to resort to simplifying assumptions. A person who has never gone to jail is assumed to be a good citizen. In general, anonymity is taken by an awarding body as sufficient evidence of good character.

Paradoxically, consideration of general character, while it complicates the job of awarding tokens, simplifies the evaluation of token holders by the general public. For every man considers himself to be a good judge of character. A man who will hesitate to evaluate another's knowledge of integral calculus will unequivocally estimate his moral worth at first meeting. This, too, will be done without any of the convenient assumptions to which awarding bodies must resort.

Needless to say, the results of this public evaluation do not always coincide with that of the awarding body. As a result, there is always a nucleus of dissatisfaction with the distribution of any award. In addition to the lay dissatisfaction there are normally two other groups with some special cause for disapproval. First, there are those who, whatever their merits, desire the award and fail to receive it. These are hardly likely to approve of the method of selection. Second, among those receiving the token are some who, regardless of their own merits, feel that the awards have been distributed too promiscuously. These, too, would have recourse to some alternate method of selection. One is reminded of the complaint of Louis XIV that every time he filled an office he created a thousand enemies and one ingrate.

These three groups, then, constitute the normal amount of dissatisfaction that any system of awarding, no matter what the care or probity of the awarders, may expect. For any particular token, of course, there may be considerably more.

Awarding bodies may fall into one of two types of error. The alpha error is the awarding of a token to someone who is unworthy. As the inappropriateness of the award is more or less evident, the dissatisfaction in the community will be more or less reflected upon the award. While awards may be given to large numbers of people, a single person in the community is likely to meet but few. It is upon these few that his evaluation of the award will be based. Insofar as these strike him as unworthy, he is likely to consider the token holder as not deserving of prestige. Too high a proportion of evident alpha errors will, in time, bring a token into disrepute.

It is also possible for an awarding body to pass over a candidate with claims comparable to those awarded—the beta error. The results of such errors are more equivocal. Their pretensions are to a degree discounted as tinged with self-interest. The possibility always exists that the awarding body is aware of some damaging datum which the candidate is at some pains to conceal from casual observation. Of course, the analogous situation for the alpha error, that the body knew of some hidden virtue, is equally possible, but people are more loath to postulate hidden virtues than hidden defects. The beta error, then, is mitigated by partial attribution of his failure to idiosyncrasy.

To compensate, however, for this discounting, beta errors tend to be more vocal. While an alpha error may speak volumes, his advertising is at least not deliberate. The beta error has little to lose by publicity and may succeed in gaining the coveted award or discrediting those who have gained it. Either represents an advancement.

In general, the higher the apparent alpha and beta errors, the less valuable will be the award. This tendency serves as one of the checks on the free action of the awarding body, it being, as we shall see, to the interest of the awarding body to prevent the complete devaluation of the token.

We may now attempt to look at the circumstances that determine the value of a particular prestige token. We may begin by considering a static situation, that is, to evaluate the prestige token at a particular point in time.

Basically, the ownership of the prestige token is a claim to the respect of those lacking the token. The utility curve for prestige tokens, unlike those of tangibles, is not completely idiosyncratic. While a person may possess a basis which he considers adequate to entitle him to the deference of others, the absence of the deference exerts considerable pressure upon him to revise his utility curve. He may, of course, continue to prize the virtue for its own sake, but he must come to recognize its inadequacy as a source of prestige.

As a result of this consensual nature of prestige, the total amount of prestige that exists in a community is a constant. Each quantum of prestige utility must be balanced by an equivalent prestige disutility or deference. The prestige may be divided—and in all known communities it is—among a number of different types. It is then necessary to ascertain both the distribution of prestige within a particular prestige type and the distribution between types.

Assuming that there are no gradations of tokens within a type, the distribution is a simple function of the number of token holders. The awarding of another token, then, decreases the value of the tokens in existence by $1/n$, where the new token holder is the nth.

Consider for a moment what the situation would be if the total value of a prestige type were constant, as in fact it is not. It would be to the interest of the token holders as a group to restrict the awarding of new tokens, since each new token awarded would represent a loss in value to them. However, the interest of each token holder, if there be more than one, would differ from that of the group. Assume he has an opportunity to award a token to a person who would be the nth token holder. The present token holder possesses $1/n - 1$ of the total prestige. In awarding the token, he loses $1/n$th of this value or $1/n \, (n-1)$ of the total value. The candidate receives this value for $(n-1)$ holders or $n - 1/n(n-1) = 1/n$th of the total. Since he receives from the bestower $n-1$ times the bestower's loss, he can well afford to repay the bestower and still profit from the transaction. Each token holder is then in a position to profit at the expense of his fellow token holders.

A sole token holder does not have this opportunity, since he has no one but himself from whom to gain an advantage. Also, if there are few token holders, their mutual dependence is evident and some combination to restrain the effects of promiscuous awarding of tokens is to be expected. Where, however, the number of token holders is large and spreads over an extensive geographical area, the common interest of the group cannot be assumed to serve as a check on the desire for advantage of each of the token holders.

There exists, however, some natural check in the ability of the total value of a prestige type to rise or fall at the expense of the value of other prestige types. Let us then consider the evaluation of the share which a prestige type enjoys of the total prestige of the society.

Insofar as the prestige type is conceived as requiring a trait rarely found in the population, the type will be highly valued. The man in the street is little likely to award great deference to a token holder if he feels that he himself is quite capable, with a little effort or luck, of acquiring a similar token. When the ownership of a token is extremely widespread, general opinion takes this as prima facie evidence that the talent required is not extremely specialized. On the whole, people agree that a chosen few have a particular talent that entitles them to deference; the acknowledgment that many or most people have claims tends to be most painful.

We have seen that prestige is assumed to include an element of effort. Where the apparent effort is great, the amount of deference accorded the prestige token holder will be correspondingly great. The apparent effort is likewise affected by the number of tokens in existence. It may generally be taken that the amount of effort which an ordinary man will expend in usual circumstances is not great. Should large proportions of the populace possess a token, it may be safely assumed that the amount of effort required is not of a high order. The notion of what constitutes the claim to prestige will accordingly be downgraded.

At any particular time, there will be a notion in general circulation of what virtues a token holder should possess. It is against this base line that holders and nonholders are compared in their usual intercourse with society. Starting from this notion, there will exist some general feeling on the amount of alpha error, that is, the number of tokens inappropriately awarded, and the amount of beta error, that is, the number of awards inappropriately withheld. With the passage of time, the estimate of error will feed back into the notion of appropriateness. Where the degree of error is too blatant, the original estimate of the value of the token will be reduced and the value of competing prestige types correspondingly enhanced.

The flexibility and the total value of the prestige type can, then, serve as a natural check to the advantage of the individual token holder in awarding tokens. He will then stand to lose not $1/n$th of the value of his own token, but $1/n$th plus or minus $1/n$th the change in total value of the prestige type which his award has caused.

Where the token is awarded to a candidate whose failure to achieve a token would constitute a beta error, the action may be presumed to enhance the total value of the prestige type, or at least to maintain it. Where, however, the candidate will be generally seen as not conforming to the notion of what a token holder could be, the awarder will suffer the loss of not only $1/n$th the original value of his token but also $1/n$th the fall in the total value of the prestige type. Of course, any award actually bestowed will be justified as the correction of a beta error.

We have until now spoken as if the only option available to an awarder is either to reject or accept the candidate. The awarder has, however, some discretion in manipulating the apparent effort that a candidate will make. Where the candidate's effort receives sufficient public notice, the possibility of alpha error is reduced. It is therefore in the interest of awarders to have the efforts sufficiently publicized, provided the degree of publicity does not discourage potential candidates. The maintenance of the proper degree of publicity is known generally as the maintenance of standards, and few conventions of awarders fail to have a session dedicated to discussion of this problem.

While the fluctuation in the total value of the prestige type is of some importance, it is not, in the ordinary course of events, of the order of magnitude to counter-balance the advantage to the awarder in extending the number of holders. There thus remains a difference between the interest of the awarder qua awarder, which is advanced by bestowal of tokens, and the interest of the awarder qua token holder, which is generally advanced by restraining bestowal.

This difference may be sufficient to convert the system to a moving equilibrium. Whether or not it does is likely to depend upon whether or not the function of awarding tokens is a full- or part-time job.

Where awarding is a part-time job, it is likely to devolve upon those token holders who have some need of the prestige that the token carries. Their interest as token holders serves to restrain them from the quick gain that is possible by the use of awarding. In such a situation, the equilibrium is likely to remain stable and the proportion of token holders to the general population is likely to remain roughly constant.

At some point in the growth of the community it will become possible for an awarder to maintain himself on the gains from bestowal of tokens. In order to do so, he will have to have a token himself, but it will not be necessary that this token maintain its full value. His interest will lie in extending the number of token holders, from which extension his revenue arises. At this point, the system will move toward the expansion of the number of token holders.

Expansion, however, is not completely willy-nilly. The fluctuation in the total value of the prestige type still remains as a partial check. While it no longer operates by threatening the value of the possession of the awarder, a loss which he is now able to afford, it does threaten the flow of candidates. If the value of the prestige type falls too sharply, candidates will be unwilling to exert themselves to acquire a token. The awarders must attempt to strike a balance at that point which assures the maximum revenue.

In fine, the rise of the professional awarder creates the conditions for a marketplace. In an unregulated marketplace, the value of a prestige token will decline with accelerating force. A point, then, should be reached at which any particular prestige token should have only negligible value. By this time alternate tokens representing the same commodity should be in currency. These alternates will have a rank order of increasing difficulty of attainment. The disappearance of a particular token will allow the alternates to fall in value and facilitate the creation of a new token to head the list. Since the imagination of man is one of the natural resources that shows no sign of being depleted, there is no reason why such a process cannot be continued indefinitely.

Movement of this sort is most visible in areas where it is the most rapid. Adjectives used in describing motion pictures demonstrate this obsolescence most graphically. A picture that is merely colossal cannot hope to attract attention. A similar process is at work in the U.S. Army, where periodic evaluation of juniors is required. At present, an officer is most emphatically disapprobated if he is rated only as excellent.

Since the actual token selected is symbolic and to a degree arbitrary, it is necessary to the maintenance of prestige only that a token exist. The nature of the token itself is largely irrelevant, although the etymological roots of a token are occasionally productive of whimsical results.

Circular behavior of this sort is possible where the acts leading to the token are unitary or internally consistent. Where, however, the acts are variegated, a selective process tends to differentiate these acts in such a fashion as to interfere with circularity.

An awarder retains his position, at least in theory, by virtue of the ability to evaluate behavior which entitles candidates to bestowal. To some extent, the awarder formalizes the requirements to aid his convenience. Certain judgmental areas remain, however. In these areas, the awarder enjoys a freer hand than he does in more esoteric areas. He then relies most heavily on the esoteric area to reduce the expenditures of acquiring a token. In fact, if the value of the token shows signs of slipping too precipitously, he may even raise the more conspicuous requirements in the hope of overshadowing the effect of lowering the more judgmental ones. During the token's progress down the ladder of values, the requirements for its acquisition develop differences in kind as well as differences in degree.

Of all of the requirements of candidacy, duration is the most conspicuous to the layman. If candidacy takes place in a spot secluded from the public eye, the proportion of the day spent in significant behavior is not readily visible. But the duration of time from the beginning of candidacy to its successful culmination in the award of the token is evident even to a child in the street.

The differentiating effect of degree of visibility is most striking on duration. As the various other behaviors which are considered significant are attenuated, duration remains constant, or even increases. Groups interested in lowering the prestige value consider maintenance of the standard of duration a convenient shield for reduction in other areas, less public. The groups interested in raising the prestige value of a token seek to extend the duration as the behavior for which the public support can be most easily marshaled.

As it happens, time is a scarce commodity. While the techniques of civilization have increased the life span to a degree, the affluent society shows its most niggardly face in increasing the production of time. Even the richest of us owns but twenty-four hours in a day.

The rather brutal fact of the short supply of time means that the failure of the requirement of duration to fall with the other requirements for investiture prevents circularity. Since high-valued tokens require the previous possession of lower valued tokens, and life is indeed short, the tokens in a prestige commodity that is declining in value may preempt the field to the exclusion of possible alternate tokens.

Since prestige requires symbolization, where the symbols have lost all significance the behavior that they mirror cannot be recognized by the community. In a small community, local notoriety may serve to accord prestige in the absence of symbols. But in a large and mobile society, strangers meet constantly and can evaluate others only by symbols. The absence of appropriate symbols means that the community cannot accord prestige to the trait that cannot be recognized.

For the community at large, the situation facilitates certain social changes. Where more primitive communities might encourage the same behavior for millennia, modern communities may shift the behaviors they delight to honor within the lifetime of a single man. The process of devaluation cannot be assumed to account for all, or even a major part, of social change; the facilitating effect is here mentioned only in passing to suggest that the results of the prestige marketplace are compatible with the tenor of present society.

But what happens to the trait, when the symbols devaluate? Nothing. Before prestige was accorded to the trait, it was distributed normally in the population. A vast societal mechanism appeared to give the curve a degree of negative skewness. The behavior that signified this trait changed in part. Increasingly, the behavior lost touch with the underlying trait. Finally, the behavior ceased to bring the approbation of the community. The trait returns to the obscurity from which it emerged. Those endowed with quantities of the trait demonstrate them as circumstances permit and inclination suggests. Those preeminent in the trait may cultivate it for the sake of its enjoyment, at some risk perhaps of being thought eccentric. Society finds a new toy.

4

Some Historical Background

Educators are wont to trace the academic enclave back to the philosophical schools of ancient Greece. Although these were undoubtedly forerunners of present educational institutions, they differed from modern institutions in a number of fundamental ways.

Greek schools were a pretty informal affair. Students came and went as they pleased. Although they often paid the philosophers who ran the schools, the terms of the contract were exceedingly vague, by present standards. No official prestige tokens were offered. The student was free to gather such prestige as he could by claiming to be a disciple of such and such a philosopher, but no credentials to back such a claim were available. Greek schools thus lacked even the rudiments of modern educational devices.[1]

During the Middle Ages, education made marked strides. Prestige tokens were introduced and contracts were formalized. By present standards institutions were still rather casual, but the outlines of modern institutions were visible.

A major turning point in the career of educational institutions was the rise of the professions.[2] As professions began to be organized, the advantage to professionals of increasing the prestige of their group was evident. It did not take long for the benefits of professional cooperation with educational institutions to become apparent. Since the institutions represented the major prestige bestower in the community, their cooperation with the professionals served to legitimate the latter group. On the other hand, the institutions did not wish, by refusal of cooperation, to foment the rise of independent sources of prestige bestowal. So mutually advantageous a combination could not be long resisted. The universities undertook to bestow a prestige token qualifying candidates for entrance into a particular profession. The professionals cooperated by making such a token a prerequisite for entering their ranks.

This expansion turned out to have incalculable value for the institution. The bestowal of tokens upon likely candidates for professional practice ruptured the previous connection of the bestowal of prestige with learning, which had so hampered the development of Greek institutions. The principle once having been established that prestige need not be connected with any specific trait, the institutions were free to develop along any particular line that seemed to promise prestige benefits. Thus the foundations for modern educational institutions were laid.

During this period, the educational enclave remained rather small. Education was seen as an elite activity. Members of the upper classes, selected by whatever means were used at the time to define upper-class membership, could contract with an educational institution if they were desirous of acquiring further prestige. Other persons might also apply, if they possessed traits considered sufficiently prestigious in the society of the time to make their contracting with an educational institution of mutual benefit. While the process was in large part a process of self-selection, the numbers remained small. Virtually all students were able to make considerable bestowals of prestige upon the educational institution. As a result of this natural limitation, the prestige of the token suffered from little or no inflationary tendencies for upward of six hundred years. This represents no mean feat when one considers that societal conditions suffered from enormous changes during this period.

The second major watershed in the history of education occurred about the 1840s. At this point the working classes began seriously to demand that their children be permitted to attend educational institutions, despite their lack of prestige to contribute to these institutions. At the time, a limited number of societies had become active to teach the manual arts to children of tradesmen and working-class parents. The response of the parents made clear their more profound knowledge of the nature of educational institutions than the would-be helpful society members. Working-class parents wanted their children taught Latin and Greek.

When the volunteer societies refused to relinquish their narrow view of what children of the working class ought to be exposed to, parents turned to the government for aid. As might be expected, from a democratically oriented government a favorable response was forthcoming. The working class represented too many votes to be ignored. Furthermore, the project fitted in very well with the interest of members of the governmental machinery. The development of educational institutions for the lower class involved the expenditure of considerable money on buying and constructing institutional plants and called for the hiring of considerable staff. Indeed, it would be an unimaginative government worker who could not put these disbursements to some good account.

Unfortunately for working-class parents, their children did not share with them the desire for augmenting prestige. As other children, they were not insensitive to the advantages of prestige, but they preferred the prestige to be garnered in peer groups. This prestige was awarded for whatever traits the peer group of the moment chose to encourage. These might include whatever skills might be considered useful for persons of that age bracket, such as the ability to twirl a yo-yo some thousand times without faltering. This divergence of interest between children and parents has not changed substantially in the last century.

As it became clear that the provision of opportunity to contract with educational institutions was not sufficient to increase sizably the probability that such contracts would actually be successfully terminated, parents turned once again to the government for intervention. It was demanded that the government commit itself to a strategy of forcing recalcitrant children to fulfill educational contracts. While official commitment was soon forthcoming, the implementation of this commitment proved subject to a number of limitations.

First, the construction of institutional plants and their staffing with sufficiently prestigious persons proved to be a rather larger job than was anticipated. Even to this day there are areas where educational facilities are inadequate to accommodate all those whom the government must force to fulfill their contract. The government soon hired special forces to compel truants to live up to their contract, but it proved too irrational to compel a truant to make his appearance at an institution too overcrowded to accommodate him.

Second, while the fulfillment of the contractual obligation of attendance was readily subject to enforcement, those students with the greatest propensity to renege on their contract proved most resistant to such contractual obligations as the maintenance of decorum. The prestigious persons who were most committed to the ideals of education proved least likely to regret the absence of the persons about whom the government was most solicitous.

Traditionally, the price of failure to fulfill a contract has been the partner's reciprocal failure to fulfill his obligation. Ordinarily, contracts have built-in maintenance features. Where, as in the case of recalcitrant children of the working class, a participant to the contract lacks interest in its fulfillment by his partner, the natural balance is lost. Children consider themselves as never having voluntarily agreed to the contract and under no responsibility to fulfill its provisions. Nonetheless, the state, committed to the fulfillment of the contract by both parties, is left with no option but to escalate to the threat of force.

In many cases this threat is sufficient, although there is little doubt that it lacks credibility. It is difficult to view the State's invoking of physical punishment or incarceration on a ten-year-old to force his attendance in an educational institution with the seriousness which the majesty of the State demands.

We have been interpreting changes in the nature of the educational enclave in terms of the demands made upon it, but these increasing demands become possible only within certain kinds of society. The most intuitively obvious correlation would be in terms of labor saturation. The increase in technology has brought us, for the first time in human history, to the point where part of the labor force can produce sufficient for the necessities and many of the commonly accepted luxuries of the community. Within the affluent society, the problem is less of finding workers than of finding jobs. Students constitute a sizable group of potential workers removed temporarily from the labor force, reducing the competition for jobs. Furthermore, faculty and administration similarly are occupied with activities that would not otherwise exist. Their salaries, as well as the cost of building progressively more elaborate physical structures, have a multiplier effect. Unquestionably, education can be defended as serving a function in a technologically advanced community.

Although technological conditions make the expansion of the educational enclave possible, they provide neither its justification nor its motivation. It is even questionable whether the technological function of education can be considered its primary function. Modern technological societies have universally abandoned the castelike class structures that characterized earlier societies. While they have continued to show the same range of gradations in socioeconomic status, these gradations have taken the form of continua rather than dichotomies or trichotomies. The key to socioeconomic classification in modern societies has been prestige. It is educational institutions that have functioned as primary bestowers of prestige.[3]

Given the fact that the striving for success in modern society tends to be concentrated in the prestige area, the claims of the working class to equal opportunity in life chances have focused upon the right to participation in the educational enclave. With the widespread demand, the justifications for educational activity which sufficed to legitimate this activity for a small elite are no longer adequate. Let us then look at the justifications which have emerged in modern society and try to trace the effects on the educational enclave that such justifications have produced.

It is generally taken for granted in the community at large that educational transactions are good. The proverbial man in the street is likely to be satisfied with this pronouncement, if he is left alone. It being the business of researchers not to let him alone, we send our imaginary interviewer to ask, why is it good? The answer is likely to be that educated people make good citizens.

It is somewhat more difficult to ascertain what good citizenship entails. Often, it is taken to mean intelligent voting. There is little doubt that citizens who have completed educational transactions vote somewhat differently. Education is one of the standard variables used in the analysis of voting results. Yet a two-party system requires a loser. It would be stretching the bounds of altruism to expect a political party to deliberately support a policy that would harm its future prospects. Republicans and Democrats alike support education. We must seek some other criterion of good citizenship

It would not be unreasonable to expect a good citizen to restrain himself from committing criminal acts. Can we expect, then, that an increase in education will lead to a diminution in crime? This seems unwarranted optimism. Certainly crimes of violence (exclusive of war crimes) are less likely to occur among those who have completed the educational transaction. Yet Sutherland's classic study of the top one hundred American corporations, run largely by educated men, shows as high a proportion of criminal recidivism as is likely among any group of corresponding size in the population.[4]

Of course, it is possible to consider a good citizen as one who does not succumb to the lure of Communism. There are some indications that this may be considered the most salient present index. Here again, there is little justification for the belief that education is an aid to good citizenship. Notoriously, the membership of Communist parties in non-Communist countries consists almost exclusively of disaffected intelligentsia. The rate of successful completion of the bargain is considerably higher than in the general population.[5]

Despite the perverse results of education in this regard, there is some reason to believe that education is intended to counteract the siren song of Communism. It has become a practice to include among the compulsory secondary subbargains a series of lectures either on the advantages of American democracy or on the disadvantages of the Soviet system—the courses are often indistinguishable. A content analysis of these subbargains would support the theory that education is intended to combat Left-wing tendencies. Nevertheless, this fails to account for the accompanying belief that a group of subbargains consisting of trigonometry, Spanish, and physics will have the same effect.

In sum, we can find no end for which the spread of education can be considered a rational means. Insofar as the spread of education has been pursued for one of the ends listed above, we must consider it an irrational means. Of course, we are not bound to the assumption that the spread of education is a means; it may be an end in itself. In this case the question of rationality does not apply, ends being outside the realm of rationality. Although we cannot be sure of the status of the ideology in regard to rationality, we can maintain nevertheless that the community favors the spread of education, whatever the reason.

In the realm of primary education, the community interest has produced clear-cut results. Since the age of compulsory attendance at educational institutions extends well beyond the point of investiture of the primary token, all children are prima facie candidates. The State having compelled participation in the transaction, it cannot in all good faith withhold the merchandise. For all practical purposes, all students receive the primary token. The withdrawal of the token, then, ceases to be a threat, and the institutional authorities have little scope to demand any behavior beyond mere attendance. The prestige value of the primary token is negligible, the assertion of a prestige claim based upon it being equivalent to the mere assertion of chronological seniority.

The faculty and authorities of primary educational institutions, being members of the previous generation or the one prior to that, have in many cases received their primary token before the effects of governmental interest had a chance to be felt. Their conceptions of the primary transaction are colored by their own experience. On occasion, they expect from candidates for a primary token the series of behaviors that were the standards of their youth. At times, this expectation creates some degree of conflict with present-day candidates.

Several factors mitigate this conflict. First, while the educational authorities are not free to withhold the token, they may refuse to continue the transaction in their institution. Since the State requires attendance, the parents of the candidate are forced to provide for the continuation of the bargain at some private institution. The costs of such a proceeding render it a hardship for poor or even middle-class persons. This weapon, however, can be used only sparingly, against individuals rather than groups.

Second, an educational theory has attained some currency which suggests the desirability of encouraging students in activities they prefer. Authorities professing such a theory are hardly tempted to confront the students with the expectations of a previous age.[6]

Third, most people, children not excepted, may be characterized as possessing a generous measure of passivity. They may be counted on to make at least token efforts to meet the expectations of those with whom they have contact. They rebel but little, though they may show a sullen lack of enthusiasm. If no challenge to the expectation of the faculty member arises to utilize the passivity in favor of some other expectation, conflict is minimal.

Finally, although the prestige token has come to have little value, the underlying trait still exists in the population. There are some, then, who spontaneously manifest those behaviors that the educational apparatus was at one time at such pains to cultivate. Since primary institutions tend to accept students from a small geographic area, and possessors of the trait are not scattered randomly in the population but cluster geographically, such students tend to be found in the same institutions. Such native propensities as these students possess may be encouraged by the example of their neighbors. The haphazard emergence of such groups, however, is seriously retarded by the attempts of educational authorities to assure heterogeneous classes, lest students with little propensity to learning feel that their own desires are less worthy than their colleagues'.

To sum up, compulsory participation in primary education has completely devalued the primary diploma, removing the token from the area of the free marketplace. Since the educator's function as awarder has become nominal, he can exercise little influence on the behavior of candidates other than such influence as the candidate encourages or the educators' personal qualities give rise to. There are still pockets of negative entropy, but the system with time should become completely based on the distribution of the propensity to learning in the population.

Compulsory primary education has, thus, disappointed both the hopes of its advocates and the fears of its opponents. The former expected that it would assure to all the benefit which primary transactions had previously afforded to a select few. The zero sum nature of prestige has precluded this possibility. The latter assumed that the desire for learning would disappear in the absence of the stimuli provided by an educational system based on prestige values. Both groups overestimated the effects of educational institutions and underestimated the resiliency of man and his capacity to choose a course of action for himself in the absence of communal reward and punishment.

Public interest in secondary education has not proceeded to the same lengths as it has in primary education. The trend is in this direction, however, and, short of a major change in public thought, it may be expected that secondary education by the next generation will be set up in the model of primary schools. For the moment, the age of compulsory attendance in school ends before the awarding of the secondary token. It is sufficiently high so that some continue their education for the short time needed to acquire the token who would otherwise refrain from the transaction. There is, as we have seen, considerable public pressure to this course, although there is little doubt that the departure of some students is greeted by educational authorities with private relief. At the present some 60 per cent of each cohort of seventeen-year-olds in the United States complete the secondary transaction. Of the 40 per cent who do not, virtually all have had some experience in secondary educational institutions and have little doubt of their capacity to acquire a secondary token. The deference accorded the possessors of a high school diploma does not seem inordinately high. Two thirds of the possessors contract for collegiate bargains, which suggests that at least these do not feel that secondary education has strained their capacity to the utmost. The characteristics of secondary education, deriving from the intermediate nature of a mixed economy, need not detain us further.

The interest of the community is voluntary, except insofar as the possession of a token is set by the State as the prerequisite for certain positions. The impact of the public interest is largely ideological and financial. Communal financial support undoubtedly makes it possible for large numbers to contract for education who would otherwise be debarred. Further, the government's position makes it possible to require certain institutions to accept all comers who have completed secondary bargains under certain conditions. The requirement, however, is so congenial to the policy of the institutions that its disappearance would affect only a negligible number of cases.

The effect of the public interest is in all respects in the direction of the devaluation of the diploma. The larger number of students means that the median possession of the trait is closer to the mean of the population. The standard of behaviors required for investiture must be lowered to a point where possession of the token is possible for persons of this degree of propensity.

Further, the larger number of holders of the token reduce the share of each in the prestige utility. The assumption that all in the population are capable reduces still further the degree of prestige claims which can be asserted on the basis of the token with any hope of recognition. The resultant devaluation reduces the effort which it is rational to make in return for the token and inaugurates a further cycle of devaluations.

Thus far, the effects of public interest have been to strengthen the hands of those groups interested in devaluation, or at least the reduction of the effort of acquiring a token. There is a further ideological effect which, if it is more subtle, is perhaps in the long run more consequential. We have seen that the most effective check to the devaluation of the token where it has been free to operate has been the self-interest of the present possessors. So long as a transaction is one of a private nature, a man is warranted in taking such actions, provided they are legal, as are necessary to protect his own interest. Where a public question is involved, while such actions are not the less common, it is expected that they be undertaken at least under the color of advancement of the public interest. Where the public interest has been defined as requiring the spread of education, such proposals as the alumni could make which would tend to limit the spread would find no public justification. The diplomate is in large measure condemned either to silence or to the onus of being part of a pressure group devoted to advancing its own interests at the expense of the public benefit. The organization of any sizable group of diplomates under such circumstances is impossible. Such action as the alumni can take is restricted to covert pressure. The possibility of the alumni acting as an effective check is thus largely neutralized.

5

The Bargain

Educational institutions prepare public statements of the terms under which they will conclude an educational contract with a potential student. These public statements, or catalogues, serve several purposes for the institution. First, by making clear the kind of educational bargain which the institution contemplates, they discourage offers of contracts from would-be partners whose range of acceptable bargain is too restricted or whose ability to contribute to the institution's prestige is too limited. Publication, then, of the general outlines of the institution's range of acceptable bargain may be considered as part of the process of dispelling uncertainty inherent in negotiation.

While this represents the formal function of the institution's catalogue and its justification, institutions are able to derive a number of secondary benefits to offset publication costs. The institution's description of the terms under which it will conclude a contract serves as notice to the public of its willingness to negotiate with all persons who meet the qualifications laid down in the description. This willingness is something of an exaggeration. Nevertheless, modern public policy demands that the selection of those partners to a contract whose collaboration is most beneficial be done in such a fashion that the principles underlying the selection not be apparent.

Finally, the opportunity to discuss the kind of educational bargains available at an institution is simultaneously an opportunity to advertise the prestige of the institution too useful to be missed. Sufficient copies of the institution's statement are therefore made to permit distribution among people whose awareness of the prestige level of the institution is desired.

Since it is a matter of common knowledge that educational institutions have prepared such statements and will make them available to prospective partners to the educational bargain upon request, along with the institution's standard form for soliciting a contract, we may consider the initial offer in a negotiation of an educational bargain to be the student's. The institution's publication is by now so formalized as hardly to be considered part of any specific negotiation. It is the student who demonstrates the first initiative in an actual negotiation. It is he who selects a potential partner or group of potential partners. The institution will accept or reject the opportunity to consummate the transaction, but the student makes the original decision. The student is confronted with a choice. If the number of possible partners were small, the choice would be relatively easy. Educational institutions are legion, however.

Still, this may or may not present a problem to the student, depending on whether he considers that there are appreciable differences between educational institutions. In the absence of appreciable differences, the student need have no concern over which partner to select. This, of course, does not mean that the institution has no concern over the decisions of potential students. Notoriously, markets where there are no appreciable differences between producers are the most threatening to the producer, for decisions are made on whimsical grounds, leaving the producers to depend on the vagaries of a choice over which he can exercise scant control. Nevertheless, it is the buyer's difficulty of choice with which we are at the moment concerned.

In the case of educational institutions, it is commonly held by students and potential students that significant differences exist. Whether this judgment is justified is moot, but irrelevant. The opinion exists, and student behavior is predictable only on the basis of this opinion. This being the case, it is rational for the student to gather certain amounts of information about institutions, for if differences exist it is reasonable that some alternatives will be better bargains than others, and that information will aid in the selection of the better bargain. Of course, the collection of all possible information on educational institutions, even if it were possible, would be irrational. For information gathering is costly in time, effort, and money, both to collect the information and to assimilate and evaluate it.

Obviously then, a point will be reached where further information gathering will be irrational; the probability is that new information will not reveal a bargain sufficiently better than the present bargain to repay the cost of acquisition. We may consider the bargain at this point as demarcating the extent of the student's range of acceptable bargain.

Suppose that we rank order all educational institutions in respect to the convenience of gathering information about them for a certain student. If he were to start with no information about the institutions other than the ease of acquiring information and no prediction about what constitutes an acceptable bargain, the rational procedure is to begin collecting information with the most convenient and to proceed along the continuum until he meets a bargain which falls within the range of acceptable bargain. Has the student minimized the cost of information? No. In all probability there is an institution somewhere beyond the range which would have been more satisfactory. If he had started from there, he would have had a lower cost of information. He does not know which institution this is, however. The probability is that the method of convenience will be more economical than any other method he will choose, given the limitations cited. This being the case, we may take the method of convenience as providing the cost of information in the absence of knowledge about educational institutions. To attempt to ascertain this cost would entail a host of technical problems, although it is possible in theory. It would vary greatly from buyer to buyer, but an average could be estimated.

Is, then, further minimization possible? We have assumed that the potential student can make no prediction about his own range of acceptable bargain. What will happen if he can? Suppose that his prediction is accurate. He is then at liberty to remove from the rank ordering of institutions those which do not meet the predicted requirement. It makes no difference what the nature of the prediction is; he may predict that he will attend no institution whose name starts with a P. The result is a saving in the cost of information gathering, since he reaches a bargain within his range after investigation of fewer institutions. To the extent that his prediction is correct, he can minimize cost.[1] Suppose, however, that he has predicted that an acceptable bargain is a small institution, but he would have opted a large institution had he proceeded by the method of convenience. In this case there would seem to be no way of estimating whether the cost of information is greater or smaller. The best that can be said is that there is no reason to assume it to be greater.

In any event, we may say that to the degree that a potential student has confidence in his ability to predict what he will consider a good bargain, it is rational to limit information gathering to those institutions that meet these criteria. We may view rational information gathering as a process of stratifying institutions along certain dimensions and gathering information in the strata which are taken to characterize acceptable bargain until such a point that the probability of improving the bargain falls below the cost of information gathering.

Given the possibility of stratifying, consider further the predicted characteristics of the good bargain which provide the basis for stratification. If these predictions are entirely idiosyncratic, there being no relationship between one student's criteria and another's, the implication for the market will be nonexistent, except for the lowering of the cost of information. On the other hand, if the criteria show a large measure of agreement, the market will be stratified. It is not necessary that students choose the same stratum to seek an acceptable bargain to produce this result, but only that they divide the institutions in a similar fashion.

As a matter of fact, there is a general agreement on the stratification in institutions. While details vary, the prevailing criterion is one of prestige. At this point the reader will have to take this for granted, the empirical research to buttress this bald assertion being lacking. It will be seen, however, to accord well with the motive for education. If the education is undertaken for prestige, it would follow logically that the transaction should be governed by the amount of prestige that one can afford to buy.

The effects of this rational consumer policy on institutions should be considered. The market is reduced to a number of submarkets, which are indirectly rather than directly competitive. Such a situation is by no means unique to education. Consider for a moment the typewriter market, which divides into an electric typewriter submarket and a manual typewriter submarket. Under present circumstances, the potential buyer in one of these submarkets is generally not a potential buyer in the other.

In general then, we may see institutions in the same stratum as competing for a number of potential students which depends on the stratum. There will be some institutions that border on two strata and others whose peculiarities make an assignment to a stratum difficult. These may be disregarded, however, in an attempt to get an overall picture of education.

Members of different strata will enjoy different advantages. We shall attempt to characterize the highest and lowest strata, with the assumption that intermediate strata will partake in varying amounts of the advantages of a high or low stratum.

The lower strata have potentially more students. This is in line with the picture for most commodities, which diagram as a flattened triangle. In general, among alternative ways of satisfying the same need, most people opt the cheaper alternative. There may be some special reason for this to occur in education, but we will not concern ourselves to justify a condition which is the rule rather than the exception in all sorts of markets.

Enjoying a larger potential clientele, institutions in lower strata can have large student bodies. This allows a lower cost per student, the utility of which is too obvious to require discussion. If educational institutions were as a rule profit-making businesses, little further would have to be said. But few if any institutions can make a profit from the contributions of the students however low they have reduced the cost per student.

Generally speaking, the amounts of money raised above student contributions, to the point of breaking even or—hopefully —better than even, come from public funds or from the bequests or contributions of private persons or corporations. In the competition for access to public funds, lower status institutions may perhaps hold their own. The larger number of partners to the transaction give them some greater claim to generosity of those who distribute public funds. The mechanics of this particular transaction will be discussed in some detail later on. In the competition for private funds, however, the high status institutions enjoy all the advantages. The benefits are more striking the higher one goes. Institutions on the higher strata are occasionally property owners of no mean degree.

From this description, it would seem that the best advice one could give a new institution would be to enter the high-status submarket. But this conclusion would be precipitate. Such advantages as are enjoyed by high-status institutions are not necessary advantages. They have been acquired by foresight or luck over a period of centuries. Moreover, the group of students for which they compete is not as elastic as it is on lower levels. A potential competing institution would find it difficult to gain a foothold. In fact, while the number of educational institutions has not shown a corresponding increase, it would seem doubtful that this state of affairs could be attributed to any lack of initiative on the part of potentially competing institutions. It would seem rather that the disadvantages of competing in the higher submarket are immediate, while the advantages are delayed and speculative.

Per contra, while there are difficulties in the establishment of an institution in the lower status submarket, the advantages precede the disadvantages. Having once obtained access to public funds, obtaining additional funds is relatively easier, the more so as the addition contributes to the education of proportionally more students. Of course, there are disadvantages to competition on the lower levels also, but on the balance the advantages would seem to outweigh the disadvantages.

The burden of this argument is that a new institution will most rationally attempt to establish itself in the low-level submarket. This in fact would seem to fit the empirical situation. It would not follow from the argument that established institutions should be prepared to make the quantum jump to a lower level. For the argument has, to this point, taken no cognizance of the equity that institutions have amassed. A degree of relative success on one level will serve to retard the movement to another level. Let us look at the mechanism which is operative.

Suppose that an established institution on one of the middle levels of status desires to become competitive on a lower level. At present, it is a candidate for a transaction with a number of potential students who have opted that particular stratum to seek information. It therefore becomes known primarily to these students. It is hoped that this number are more than compensated by the large number of potential students opting to acquire information about institutions on a lower level. But the datum that the institution is now on a lower level does not reach these potential students immediately. Thus, the jump down to a lower level requires the institution to absorb an immediate loss.

Furthermore, present students and alumni have, respectively, begun and completed a transaction based on the aquisition of prestige which the institution is now devaluating. They may be expected to react unfavorably. In the case of students, they may opt to transfer the bargain to another institution. The number of students with enough initiative to carry out such a proceeding is, however, small enough to cause no concern. They will, however, succeed in spreading the news to those quarters where its reception is least desired by the institution. The alumni represent to the institution largely a source of possible funds. To the degree that such actual or potential funds exist, the alumni have power to interfere with a policy of devaluation. To the degree that they gain, they are motivated to exercise this power.

These drawbacks to the quantum jump to a lower level apply only to a radical policy of movement. The alternatives are not limited to this action. It is possible to change the level over a period of years through a policy of small changes. This allows an institution to garner the advantage of a lower level without suffering the immediate disadvantages. It may accord progressively warmer welcome to potential students interested in lower prestige levels of education, without indicating to those interested in a higher level that any change in policy is contemplated. In sum, rational institutions will approach their aims as the porcupine approaches his love, circumspectly.

From the argument it might seem that the market should show a constant prestige slippage on the middle and lower levels with increasing differentiation between upper levels and middle and lower levels, the upper levels being hesitant to risk the accrued advantages of upper-level fund raising. But the facility in fund raising that the upper level enjoys is not a function of their absolute prestige, but of prestige relative to other institutions. The slippage of the middle level allows the upper level to fall without risk, so long as it does not fall below the prestige of competitors in the adjacent stratum. Upper levels can thus enjoy in modified form their share of an expanding market.

To sum up, the students' rational attempts to minimize the expenditure of information seeking has stratified the market. The nature of the resulting strata is such that a descent to a lower stratum promises reasonably secure advantages to the institution in the foreseeable future, while ascent can promise only speculative gains over a longer period. The immediate dangers involved in a sudden drastic descent cause institutions to proceed slowly. Although some institutions attempt to descend in order to compete with a different set of institutions, others descend because it is possible to reap the advantages of staying with the present set of competitors. In either event, since the considerations tend to apply with approximately equal force to all institutions, all descend at approximately the same rate. Thus the relative standings of institutions tend to remain fairly constant, while the absolute prestige tends to fall.

This picture of the market emerges from analysis of long-range plans to shift from submarket to submarket. Decisions on pricing are likely to be affected by day-to-day considerations vis-à-vis competitors in the same submarket, however. We must investigate the situation in this area to determine rational policy on a daily basis. Let us then return to the question of student information gathering.

We have followed our potential student through the step of stratifying educational institutions. He is now seeking information about a set of institutions of approximately the same prestige. The return for his expenditure will then be approximately the same whichever one of the institutions he selects. However, the information he gathers may show that differential expenditures may suffice to gain this return. The rational student will select the institution, *ceteris paribus,* which requires the least expenditure.

There is an element of paradox in this process. The stratification by prestige is based to a marked degree on the assumed efforts of the student body. It is a generally held opinion that high-prestige institutions require greater expenditures of time, effort, and money on the part of their students. To what extent this opinion is realistic need not concern us. It is sufficient to indicate that the prestige of institutions is dependent on the appearance of requiring a high expenditure. Yet, having selected a stratum, the student proceeds to shop around to find the lowest expenditure possible. This paradoxical behavior is not limited to the educational transaction. For example, purchasers of cars select a stratum characterized by high expense, yet seek to purchase an expensive-looking car as cheaply as possible. The behavior is understandable on the basis of a nice distinction. Prestige is dependent not on the expense, but on the appearance of expense. An inexpensive purchase that appears more expensive than it is satisfies both criteria neatly. In a situation of perfect information, there would be no discrepancy between actual expenditure and apparent expenditure. But the real world is not characterized by certainty. In education, particularly, the large number of institutions and the series of complicated subtransactions place information beyond the range of casual inquiry. The gap between real and apparent expenditures is large enough to allow considerable room for sharp selection to repay the effort of information gathering.

Since the potential student is motivated to minimize expenditures, competition between institutions in the same submarket are largely oriented to reduction of the expenditure required. The short-range effects of competition, therefore, tend to push the institution in the direction that must lead in the long run to the reduction of prestige. But, as we have seen, this is the direction in which the institutions desire to travel. The question, however, is one of speed. Too great sensitivity to short-range considerations may reduce the prestige of an institution precipitately. Rational policy then constrains the institution to have a care that the pressure of competition is resisted to a degree. In general, institutions try to stay in roughly the same or a slightly lower position relative to other institutions.

The argument thus far has considered the effect of an institution on other institutions and of potential students. As we shall see in further chapters, the institution must consider the effect of its own student body. Students are highly motivated to minimize expenditures and possess the leisure and ingenuity to invent new methods of achieving this end continually. The result of these endeavors is to threaten the prestige of the institution with a rapid descent. The unchecked state of institutional prestige is likely to be a dizzy descent. In order to prevent this occurrence, the institution is continually required to make strenuous efforts to maintain its prestige. These strenuous effects are, preferably, conspicuous.

Naturally, nothing could be more devastating to the institution than the success of its avowed policy of maintaining prestige. The likelihood of such an untoward pass is negligible. Meanwhile, the institution is credited with the good intentions that so often pass as legitimate currency in our society.

In considering the educational bargain, we have examined the method by which the student selects an educational institution and the implications that the mode of selection has on the prestige value of the diploma, assuming for the time that the economic goods that the student contributed were convertible into a single standard. This is something of a simplification. Let us reexamine the beginnings of the educational contract, paying attention to the various utilities that the student may contribute as his share of the bargain.

The student is exchanging money and effort for a more or less prestigious token. The choice of a partner is influenced both by the price the student is willing or able to pay and the amount of prestige he demands and by the form in which he prefers to pay his price.

Price can be analyzed into money and effort. The amount of money that an education costs can vary within certain limits. It is almost never zero. While tuition at certain institutions is free, and while subsidies are at times available to cover living expenses, it is rare that the student would be unable to earn more in the labor force for the time that is spent on his education. It is perhaps only in a depression that the monetary expense of education can be zero for any appreciable group of students, under the assumption that a particular student would be unemployed if not in school. With minor exceptions, therefore, it can be considered that the student agrees to some at least temporary monetary loss. The existence of competitive institutions tends to keep the monetary expense within certain limits, since an institution raising the price too high tends to lower the number of students who attend, with consequent financial difficulties for the institution.

The financial state of the student acts as a ceiling. Where a person is unable to afford the expense of even free education, he is debarred from becoming a student. Where he can afford the most expensive education, all schools are, in the absence of other disabilities, open to him. Where his financial state is somewhere in between, some schools are available and some are not.

The ability to pay is not ascertainable by any simple examination of the income or assets of the candidate or his family, but is in part a function of the willingness of the candidate to incur the expenses of an education, that is, the utility value of the diploma to him. Case histories are replete with tales of students or their families suffering years of drudgery for an education, while families more comfortably situated have vetoed education as prohibitively expensive. Ability to pay, therefore, must be conceptualized as being determined by whether assets reach far enough down on the utility scale for a particular student to include any, some, or all possible educational arrangements.

Even where any institution can be afforded, however, there may exist a rational desire to minimize spending. All other things being equal, a less expensive institution will be preferred. While all other things are never equal, impoverishment or lack of interest will make them seem so. Where marginal differentiation falls below the threshold of perception of inequalities, then, the less expensive institution will be preferred.

It is also expected of the student that he maintain the value of the diploma. There are various ways in which this is possible. If he is possessed of sufficiently prestigious lineage, his simple presence at an educational institution is considered to add luster to the diploma. The value of such prestige is to some degree relative. What is an honorable lineage in a small town in Kentucky, may be small beer in Milwaukee. Those whose lineages enjoy national prestige have access to all institutions on the basis of title; those whose families enjoy only local notoriety must confine themselves to local institutions, if they are to trade on the full value of their patronyms.

It has become the custom of educational institutions to compete with one another in jousts of sport, the victors in such tourneys being considered to have added to the value of their diplomas at the expense of the value of the losers' diplomas. Such indications of the excellence of education as enemy goal posts are therefore highly prized by institutions. Students who show the promise of being champions in such contests of academic prowess as football, basketball, or rowing are enabled by their efforts to perfect these skills to reflect credit on the name of their alma mater. Students so gifted are so rare that no major institution admits to having enough of them. If they have sufficient ability, therefore, they can obtain access to the most prestigious institutions, even in the absence of other bargaining points.

In general, the superordinate position of the institution vis-à-vis the student renders it unnecessary for the institution to solicit students. Academic custom, as well as a rational consideration for the maintenance of the status of the diploma, has made such solicitation undignified. Nevertheless, the strong competition between institutions in respect to tournaments, the short supply of student champions, and the seriousness with which the institution views the effects of its standing at the lists on the market value of the diploma have led to some relaxation of the rigor of the restrictions in this area. Institutions are permitted to seek talent where they can find it.

The organization of nationwide tourneys requires a degree of formalization. The number of institutions competing can be increased only by fixed quantum jumps. Further, participation by an institution in these contests requires a sizable investment in time and money, sufficient to remove many of the smaller institutions from active competition. It may thus come about that a student champion may find easy access to high-prestige institutions where he would fail to merit even a second consideration from institutions of lower prestige.

The presence of some students of marked intellectual ability is also considered conducive to the prestige of institutions. Although these are not so in demand as persons of lineage or student champions, some minimum is considered respectable. Students of this stripe have, unless barred by financial considerations, access to virtually any institution.

A candidate whose claims to lineage, championship, or intellectual prowess are modest is by no means deprived of the possibilities of education, though his range of possible institutions is to varying degrees curtailed. As long as he gives no evidence of too peculiar a behavior or too blatant an inability to meet collegiate norms, he may, if he has the financial ability, expect to be educated.

A candidate's assets, as we have seen, set limits to the range of institutions he can realistically consider as potential partners. Within these limits, there are often many institutions. How does the candidate choose the institution he prefers? He does this by assigning a marginal utility value to the prestige of the various institutional diplomas and to the expenditure of his various assets. If he places a larger value on the marginal utility of the more prestigeful education than on the expenditure of his assets, he seeks those institutions with the highest prestige to which his assets entitle him. If, on the other hand, he places a higher value on his own expenditure of money and labor, he seeks an institution of lower prestige value than the best that he can afford.

Up to this point the student has been engaged in making his choice of institutions, eliminating from consideration those to which his assets would not entitle him. When he begins to consider application to an institution, it is necessary for realistic action that he estimate the probability of acceptance by any particular institution. Here uncertainty begins to play a role. While a candidate may have some idea of the utility values an institution places on his assets, it is unlikely that his estimate of them and the institution's will agree exactly. Further, the institution's utility curve is interpreted through a bureaucracy, which blurs the simple idealized utility curve that the institution is trying to set up. In addition, the student is likely to know only in the grossest terms what his rank order is among the applicants that season, since he cannot know the number or composition of the applicants except by general repute. Still further, the institution may be balancing its student body among geographic or ethnic groups or using some idiosyncratic consideration.

There are several means by which the student can cope with uncertainty. He can seek specialized information, through published reports or the services of a counselor. This involves some effort. It is often not too helpful. Institutions rarely commit to publication all their criteria by virtue of the fact that they may not be clearly formulated even to the bureaucracy, and, when formulated, are often in conflict with the institution's need for good public relations. For example, if an institution is interested in offering monetary aid to champions or intellectuals, it may feel that revelation of its extreme need will jeopardize its standing. It then prefers to use the less fruitful method of recruiting by discreet inquiry to the risk of publishing its criteria.

The uncertainty concerning the institution's behavior is not limited to its criteria for acceptance, but extends to the demands it makes during the educational process. If anything, there is even less certainty here, for the institution is able, as we shall see, to change its requirements years after the acceptance of an application. The candidate must not only estimate the probable expenditure of money and effort on the basis of the institution's present policy but must evaluate the probable extent and direction of change in the institution's policy over the next four years.

Therefore, rational practice on the part of the candidate often dictates multiple applications. Wherever the student is sophisticated enough to rationalize his marketing behavior, such a procedure is likely.

Multiple application is, in fact, the practice over the large range of institutions. Exceptions occur at the upper and lower prestige limits. Where a student is possessed of assets so valuable that he can be sure an institution will assign them a utility value commensurate with his own estimation, he may safely apply only to the institution of his choice. At the other end, a student of most mediocre assets or pronounced diffidence may choose an institution that is either of so low a prestige to assure his success or of some compulsion to accept all comers meeting some legal standard. Here, too, we may consider the student as having obviously more than enough assets to make the institution's action predictable, although this may be due to the student's foregoing the option of applying to more prestigious institutions where his candidacy would be more dubious.

Assuming that a candidate has selected an institution as a possible participant in his education, he will then obtain from the institution a series of questions, pertinent and impertinent, concerning his past life, present abilities, and future intentions. Further, the application is likely to include a request for the opinions of several teachers or substantial citizens on various questions pertaining to the candidate. This requirement seems to be of purely ritual significance. It is only the candidates of least repute who cannot find several men of substance willing to inscribe the formulae. Only the most perverse of individuals would qualify his approbation by hint of inadequacy. The signers are likely to be even less known to the university than to the candidate. In general, the necessity for the proceeding is connected with the development of administrative bureaucracy, and has, in fact, little to do with the candidate.

The candidate is further required to submit one or more short essays describing the important events in his life or why he has chosen that particular institution to attend. While the literary productions which ensue are of some interest to the institution, it is largely for the purpose of screening out misfits. The candidate's response is likely to be a function of his character and his certainty concerning the institution's intentions. Where the student is of the unobtrusive modal type, the essays are likely to show nothing more harmful than an inability to cope with the English language, a peccadillo that most institutions view most tolerantly. Where, on the other hand, the student is less conventional or more serious, he may, in the absence of temperate advice or a preternatural awareness of the makeup of institutions, be tempted to introspect the crucial points of his life or aspirations. Any severe indications of such a disposition can be expected to subject the candidate to a stressful interview, if not to rejection out of hand.

Assuming the candidate to have passed these hurdles, and to have provided the transcripts of all his academic and extracurricular activities, he is now in for a prolonged wait. If he has a paranoid disposition, he is likely to see in this some reflection on his particular application. Although this occurs in some cases, the delay is more likely to be the inevitable effect of bureaucratic operation. It is to be expected that the student's application will be officially accepted within several weeks after the term has begun, although later acceptances are recorded. In most of these cases, some tentative and unofficial agreement is reached to allow the student to begin school during the interim. In actual fact, the length of the delay is largely due to the student's unseemly hurry to begin negotiations. Many candidates submit applications as early as a year in advance, in the mistaken hope of receiving an early answer. This does much to encourage the institution to make inquiries that it would otherwise deem unessential, it being the nature of administrators to avoid any premature decisions. The general effect on all but the extremely sophisticated candidate is debilitating. All things, however, have an end. We may assume the candidacy safely accepted.

Ordinarily, then, a bargain is struck between educational institution and student within a single round of negotiations. The institution's official price is public, available for the price of a postcard or a visit. The prospective student makes an offer. The institution accepts or rejects. As far as striking the bargain goes, there the matter normally ends. Neither party makes counteroffers. No one escalates into a power dimension. No one solicits government intervention. The entire process of bargaining is handled in a summary, even cursory manner.

For the institution, the conclusion of a bargain, with some few exceptions listed above, is a matter of no great import. It is obviously to the advantage of the institution to handle its negotiations in as efficient a form as possible. In practice, this involves the standardization of contracts. In this respect, the educational institution does not differ from other bureaucracies. Organizations that negotiate hundreds or thousands of contracts of comparatively small size are little likely to waste much time haggling over the terms of each. While a good deal of flexibility is left in negotiation for the hiring of upper-echelon personnel, and the sale or purchase of large quantities of goods in a single transaction, more routine bargains are rigidly standardized.

From the point of the student, the same considerations do not hold. He is entering into a contract, the fulfillment of which will occupy several years. A successful counter-offer is conceivably of considerable advantage. The rarity of such occurrences is, at first blush, somewhat surprising. When one compares the simplicity of negotiation of the educational bargain with the complexity of bargains of approximately equal value in other enclaves, such as, for instance, the purchase of a car, the discrepancy is still more conspicuous.

The simplicity of educational bargaining seems to be a function of the minimal use of power. The student is ordinarily the weaker party by a considerable measure. Escalation into the power dimension appears both hazardous and unproductive. Nor does the probability of successful manipulation of intervention by a single student appear high. At this stage the potential student has not yet made contact with other students in the same institution. Collective action is, therefore, also unfeasible. Unless a particular prospective student happens to enjoy some particular power advantage, the most rational course open to him is to initiate negotiation with other institutions.

As is predicted by our model, the failure of negotiations to escalate into the power dimension does not indicate the absence of effect of disparities of power on the point at which the bargain is struck. The relative power positions of institution and student have already functioned to contract the range of acceptable bargain for the former and to expand it for the latter. As a result, few students end up with a bargain that they would have seriously considered had they felt they had any say in the matter. We may leave to the psychologists the analysis of the personal effects of such a situation.

Given the widespread knowledge of the relative power positions at the time of negotiation of the educational bargain, the prospective student's range of acceptable bargain will have expanded to the point where he is unlikely to refuse all contracts. It is this rigidity on the part of the student, combined with the institution's drive for efficiency, which makes possible the high degree of standardization of educational bargains.

6

The Student's Fulfillment of Contract

$\mathbf{H}$aving negotiated his contract with the educational institution, the student is now committed to its fulfillment. As we have seen from the discussion of the nature of educational bargains, the student's primary commitment is to participation in activities that lend prestige to the educational institution. This participation may be, to varying degrees, onerous. In any event, these participations tend to limit the extent of the participation of the student in other enclaves. For most students, interaction in other enclaves is not tied to previous contract. Thus, there are varying advantages to be gained through participation in these other enclaves. Within the educational enclave, per contra, the student's advantages are largely limited to a prestige token to be awarded by the educational institution in fulfillment of its part of the contract.

The situation, however, is somewhat more complex. Although the institution's fulfillment of its contract is in theory contingent upon the student's prior fulfillment of his contractual obligations, contracts have their elasticities, as we have seen. I will discuss in a later chapter the educational strategies of educational institutions and the manner in which their pursuit of their own interest produces elasticities. Suffice it for the moment to say that the elasticity of the educational contract is not zero.

This being the case, students are motivated to minimize the participation contractually called for beyond the point which an unsympathetic reading of the contract terms would indicate. It would be beyond the scope of this work to deal with all of the possible minimizations that might occur to the fertile mind of the student. I will try, however, to sketch out roughly the main area of minimization.

The danger involved in minimization is obviously that of exceeding the elasticity of contract at some particular point and risking the accusation of breach of contract and subsequent renegotiation under unfavorable terms. It is of great utility to be aware of the exact extent of elasticity at a particular point. A good part of educational conversation among the students is devoted precisely to this topic. As in other areas, specialization tends to produce experts. These may be of great use to fellow students. While in point of fact the general situation in regard to elasticity is well known, there always remain some details of information available to repay the devotion of those who dedicate themselves to finding them.

In consideration of the general process of negotiation we have seen that bargainers frequently resorted to the use of persons with special technical information or competence. Such services are, of course, costly and are used by those who have sufficient investment to safeguard and sufficient resources to permit them the luxury of purchasing such ancillary skills. Students tend to be somewhat limited in both investment and resources, so the technical development in the field has not kept pace with the specialization that has occurred in contractual negotiations in other enclaves. Only where associations of students have developed have the conditions been propitious to the development of the field. Most students pursue their minimization with no more help than can be afforded by informal consultations with those known to enjoy special competence. Let us look at some of the minimizations.

Most of the student's contractual obligations require his presence, at stated intervals, at appointed locations. Minimizing the number of appearances is obviously beneficial. While the appearance or nonappearance of any particular student is of no great import to the institution, the simultaneous nonappearance of large numbers tends to be conspicuous. Prudence suggests that the nonappearance of students be staggered. In situations of comparative inelasticity, the relative infrequency of nonattendance allows for this solution with a minimum of formal organization. In situations of higher elasticity, a fair amount of cooperation and coordination among students may be necessary to maximize minimization.

Given the nature of quasi-societies, the fulfillment of a particular contract within an enclave need not preclude the simultaneous participation in other enclaves. Depending on the nature of the particular enclave, it may, of course, impose certain limitations. Students interested in practicing hobbies during the period of their participation in obligatory attendance may or may not be able to indulge their desire, depending on their hobby. Whittling, for example, is feasible; singing is not. In general, hobbies that tend to disturb the indulgence of other educational participants in their hobbies will not be permitted.

A major requirement of the university is periodic testing. The student is required to achieve certain grades in these tests, depending on the status of the subject, the student's grades on other tests, and the particular policy that the institution is pursuing. Generally, adherents of standard educational theory have assumed that the student will be accumulating information of various sorts continually during the interval from test to test. His preparation for the test should consist of a simple recapitulation of the information he has amassed. He is expected to retain the information more or less permanently. The testing is assumed to have no effect on the information acquired or the subsequent recall, much as an experiment in physics, before the advent of quantum theory, was assumed to have no effect on the object tested.

In point of fact, such a behavior on the part of the student would be irrational. It involves, first, expenditure of much time and effort, only a small part of which he is actually tested on. Any particular datum has a utility to the student proportional to the probability of its being required to answer a question in a test. Second, a student amassing information several weeks before a test is likely to forget the information unless he restudies it. Studying just before a test therefore cuts down the expenditure for the information considerably. The difficulty from the student's point of view is knowing on which information he will be required to answer questions. A student who knows just what his quiz is concerned with can therefore make a large reduction in his expenditure at no cost to himself.

In contrast to other areas of uncertainty, the uncertainty concerning the questions in the test is one with which the student is very familiar, it being a small, highly formalized problem that the student meets recurrently and that he is highly motivated to solve. As a result, many solutions have emerged through the years. These are passed along from student to student and are rediscovered when forgotten. Let us look at some of these methods for minimizing effort.

The simplest procedure for ascertaining the questions of a small test is to ask the person constructing the test. Testwise students adopt this procedure almost as a matter of form, even where previous experience with the instructor indicates the valuelessness of the answer. The instructor may refuse the information, wishing the students to acquire more information than the test taps. He may often deliberately or inadvertently mislead the students. Even where the response is correct, as far as it goes, an instructor is unlikely to give a student a sufficient idea of the relative weights that various bits of information possess. Often his answer is as casual as "It's on the last three chapters."

Where the negligence or the sadism of the instructor prevents the student from acquiring a good idea of the utility of various bits of information, recourse may be had to other data.

Often copies of past tests of the same instructor are available. Since these are recognized to be of value, tests are often kept for many years, individually or in such student clearing houses as fraternities or clubs. Where copies of five previous years' examinations by a professor on the same information can be obtained, a realistic estimation of the probability of any datum being required is possible. The probability is that some 60 per cent of the test will consist of questions asked at least three times in the past five years. If the student prepares himself on every question asked more than one time, he may expect to pass without any difficulty. Where tests are standardized over a large area, for example, Regents Tests in New York, copies of previous tests are published, and studying from these is standard procedure.

Where these possibilities for minimizing effort are unavailable, the rational student will refer to a review book. Most textbooks officially prescribed for courses are uneconomical for use as study guides. They are highly likely to contain more extraneous information than utilitarian data and, still more important, are unlikely to evaluate the probable utility of each datum. On the other hand, the review book is designed to contain only those data with a high probability of inclusion in the test and is typographically arranged to call attention to the most utilitarian of these. Use of a review book, then, represents a major saving in time and effort. Whenever a course is commonly given in colleges and the widespread value of a review book is apparent, there is likely to be one published. These are regularly available to almost all students and enjoy a great popularity.

There is still one other method of evaluating the probability of any particular item being required for the test, namely, getting a copy of the test. Since tests are often mimeographed or printed some time before their use, it is occasionally possible to obtain a copy in time to prepare for the examination. Although this is most economical, the saving must be balanced by the possibility of detection and an evaluation of the results of exposure. Both of these factors vary considerably between institutions and within them. Since widespread knowledge of acquiring copies of a test is likely to injure future usefulness of the method, any estimation of the frequency of occurrence is difficult. Successful maneuvering in this area is repeated from student to student in anecdotal form, where considerations of future usefulness no longer come into play. Legend suggests that few institutions are free from at least occasional minimization by this method, but the well-known tendency of oral reports to become embellished in the telling makes any real estimate precarious.

Even assuming that the student has, by judicious evaluation, selected only those items of information that he will prepare for in the examination, some time and effort is needed to commit these to memory. Here, too, the rational student can minimize, however. Although standard educational theory assumes that tests measure the information stored in the student's memory, they do, in fact, only measure the information available to him at the time of testing. It is possible to make good use of this discrepancy between theory and empirical fact.

Several sources of information may be available to the student during the time of testing. The student may have access to textbooks or review books. While these require little or no expenditure to prepare, they have several disadvantages. They are rarely constructed with the view to this purpose, and the student may waste much valuable test time in seeking the relevant information, particularly if he has had no opportunity to familiarize himself previously with the locations of the needed data. These books also tend to be bulky and cumbersome and call an undesirable degree of attention to the students using them. As the institution is on occasion forced, from various considerations of its own, to make at least a token attempt to prevent the use of such substitutes for memory, discretion is often at a premium.

The use of a notebook summarizing professorial lectures on the subjects avoids some of these disadvantages. Since the size of the notebook is left to the student's option a conveniently small notebook is feasible. Further, items with a high probability of being useful may be identified easily. Where the student uses his own notebook, the fact that he has written it tends to give him some familiarity with the contents and reduces the time necessary to locate desired items. There are, however, other disadvantages that limit the popularity of such a minimizing procedure. First, a complete notebook requires attendance of many classes and some sustained attention, both of which are likely to be generally unutilitarian. Second, notebooks are in script, which is likely to be rather illegible, particularly under stressful conditions.

The various disadvantages of locating information from these sources has given rise to the practice of preparing special summaries for use during testing. These are generally designed to cover the information most likely to be required and are prepared with a view toward compactness and easy access to information. Where official institutional policy frowns on the use of such utilitarian devices, many ingenious caches for these summaries—or crib sheets as they are technically called—have been devised. Shirt cuffs, handkerchiefs, and wristwatch cases are among the most common portable locations; lavatories provide storage for larger productions. Although the use of these summaries in an inconspicuous manner is at first difficult, many if not most college students have sufficient experience so that casual reference to them is likely to escape the notice of all but the most determined and suspicious observers. Crib sheets, although they have the advantage of convenient and discreet access to information, do require an expenditure of time and effort to prepare to the degree that their composition on occasion requires scarcely less time than would memorization of the material contained. Even where the net saving in time is small, however, the summaries do provide more security for the student, the possibility of defective memory being eliminated.

All the minimization thus far discussed has taken no cognizance of the presence of other students during testing. In practice, testing is usually conducted in groups. It may be expected, from the theory of probability, that some of the students will have available information to which others do not have direct access. This marginal information will then have a premium value for the student who possesses it. If he is lacking other data, he may well exchange one datum for another, so long as the exchange is conducted with the necessary modicum of discretion. Information, however, is not the only medium of exchange available. Students may choose payment in cash, favors owed, popularity, or such other utility as fancy dictates. In practice, nonutilitarian considerations do come into play at this point, and a student may distribute information from motives of affection or charity, the more so as the utility of such information is obviously highly perishable.

Techniques of transfer of information vary. Oral transmission is most convenient where feasible. Where this method is precluded, the copying or exchanging of answer sheets is often utilized. Like oral transmissions, this method leaves no permanent record. The risk is confined to the time when answers are in some position other than the one postulated by educational theory. Both of these forms of written transmission are somewhat irrational for the sender, except in the case of true-or-false or multiple-choice tests, in that he is to some degree at the mercy of the receiver's ability to paraphrase. Where the receiver's ability is known to be limited, the sender is rationally motivated to do his own paraphrasing, preferring the risk of providing evidence of collaboration to the risk of detection by literary analysis.

All the methods heretofore examined for minimizing effort by virtue of the discrepancy of educational theory and practice are standard practice for all types of institutions, but there are some minimizing procedures specific to large institutions. Tending to take advantage of the impersonality of the larger institutions, these involve the substitution of some more knowledgeable student for the student required to be tested. Where the situation permits so elegant an economy, knowledgeable students are often at a premium during examination times and transiently enjoy the popularity usually accorded only to prestigious students or champions.

It is difficult to estimate the extent of minimization practices of the standard types outlined or of the host of specialized techniques that arise wherever opportunity and ingenuity permit. Both understanding of the rationality of such procedures and familiarity with the collegiate scene suggest that some varieties of these practices are well-nigh ubiquitous. So far as is known, no systematic study of utilitarian practices has been undertaken.

Analysis to this point has concentrated on the rational acquisition of relevant information and has disregarded the rationality of differential methods of presentation. We shall proceed to remedy this lack.

Where testing is conducted by means of true-or-false questions or multiple-choice, little variation in presentation is possible. The time-honored device of using ambiguity, that is, making a letter that can be taken as a "t" or as an "f" or sloppily erasing, with the option of explaining when information is more easily available, is usually reserved for new teachers. Even these are not unlikely to recall the device from student days.

Where essay answers are required, judicious consideration of modes of presentation permits much economy in the time and effort of information gathering. Short answers can be mechanically evaluated; longer essays must be considered in some non-mechanical fashion. We may expect that some bias on the part of the evaluator will enter. When they are behaving according to the canons of maximum rationality, therefore, testwise students will consider the answers required of them not in the abstract but as exercises in other-directedness or empathy. The rational student will ask "How would the evaluator answer the question?" While this reformulation places the student in a more operational position, he has not yet exhausted his possible minimizing procedures. Certain generalizations can be made concerning the nature of faculty and can be tried wherever there is nothing to indicate that the particular professor departs from the norm. For example, almost invariably the value of an essay is considered directly proportional to its length. It is thus economical for the student to continue writing at as fast a clip as possible, the probability being that time taken out to think of a more relevant answer will not be repaid in a higher mark. While there are instances in which professorial discouragement of illegibility set some limit to the productiveness of the student, more often a degree of illegibility is a decided asset. Where the professor is confronted with a series of paragraphs in which relevant words are legible but the statements made can be decoded only by the exercise of time and effort, the professor, being rational, usually gives the student the benefit of the doubt.

In general, a relevant essay is more likely to be evaluated highly than an irrelevant essay, but the latter is by no means debarred from consideration. It must be kept in mind that the degree of attention likely to be focused on evaluating any particular question is small. Where the student lacks information for a relevant answer, he may rationally write an essay which only by dint of concentration can be distinguished from an informative one. Beginning with a restatement of the question, the adroit student leads the discussion to an area where he has information at his disposal. Few will recall, after reading two or three pages, what the original question was. The possibility of answering questions by misdirection allows much saving of time and effort in preparing for tests. The student can select several topics and become more familiar with them than would be possible if larger masses of information were required. Where a sufficient number of clusters of information are at hand, the probability is high that several can be introduced.

Although these and other rational procedures for presentation of data on a test are readily available, their practice, with the notable exception of lengthening of presentation, is limited by the social distance between faculty and students. In the absence of widespread knowledge of academic habits, professors are often conceptualized as poring over student productions, weighing each point in some metaphorical scale of justice, and assigning a mark only after the most lengthy soul-searching. Actually, such a conception offers little basis for rational action.

In addition to or as a substitute for testing, institutions may require preparation by the student of a paper. Standard educational theory considers that the student will carefully think through some topic or problem, do such research as is necessary to obtain information, and formulate the results in clear and precise English. Such a proceeding would require what is often an irrational amount of time and effort. Alternative and more economical procedures are often adopted.

Since writing a paper involves presentation of information, the minimizing techniques discussed in relation to answering essay questions in testing apply here with minor modifications. Speed, although desirable, is not at such a premium as during testing. Verbosity, illegibility, and misdirection are as advantageous in writing a paper as in taking a test, however.

In addition to these minimizing techniques, advantage can be taken of the less constrained circumstances under which papers are written. For one thing, it is taken for granted that the formulation of the paper is the student's own invention *ab initio*. Since the task is to some varying degree onerous and time consuming, recourse may be had to plagiarism or research. By time-honored student definition, these are distinguished by the fact that the latter requires more than one source. In both cases reference is had to published material. Some care, therefore, is usually taken by more experienced students to select more obscure works, the probability of whose recognition is attenuated correspondingly. Where the source material has a distinctive style, it is often paraphrased to blend with collegiate norms.

Where published material is used, irrelevancy may become a problem. When a short composition is required, of course, some relevant introductory paragraphs can be added with satisfactory results. It is often a convenience to have a paper tailor-made for a specific assignment. This is not as difficult as it may seem; instructors commonly repeat assignments from year to year, and different instructors often assign passably similar subjects for compositions. Past papers are therefore a premium commodity. A student with a fair number of friends—they themselves having friends of their own—can locate a previous composition quite adequate to the purpose in cases where the assignment is not too unusual. Student clearing houses usually maintain a collection of papers that can serve as a ready-made library. Although some of these must on occasion be brought up to date by substitution of a more modern reference, their past performance provides some guarantee of their usefulness.

Occasionally it is necessary to have a composition written. Here the economy cannot be as marked. Still, the rational student will manage some saving by the use of specialization. Within any community, there are individuals who by disposition or practice become proficient in every skill regularly used in that community. The skill of writing compositions is no exception to this rule. A skilled artisan can turn out a composition as acceptable, or more acceptable, than the work of the average student in only a fraction of the time. Where the student possesses items of value sufficient to compensate the artisan for his time, labor, and to some extent the previous time and labor spent in acquiring the skill, the elements for a mutually advantageous arrangement are to hand. The pricing arrangements, economic theory would suggest, will be less dependent on a fair return than on the laws of supply and demand. The small number of such occasions and the inability to mass produce prevent the rise of a full-time occupation of composition writing, however.

Considerations that tend to keep composition writing at an amateur status apply only to the usual small efforts required. It has become the custom at universities to require a larger composition for the granting of more advanced prestige tokens. These are subject to some degree of supervision by the faculty and are, at least nominally, expected to explore some new area of learning. The use of published works or previously written compositions is by dint of this fact curtailed. Since the effort is greater and more time consuming, a degree of professionalization has emerged among thesis writers.

The professionalization of this occupation has been considerably abetted by historical circumstances. The thesis was originally intended to be a requirement that the student have published a composition meeting certain educational norms. To a large degree, publishers are independent of the educational system and select works to be published by rational considerations of their own, based more on their estimation of the probable sale of the volume than on the educational advantages it affords the author. Some institutions have gone into the publishing business in the hope of combining the profits of publishing with the advancement of their students and the building of school prestige. Even these, however, cannot hope to cope with the large number of students whom the institutions desire to educate. The requirements have, therefore, become relaxed to permit the publication to be a symbolic one. The student may, at his own expense, prepare a certain number of typed copies or microfilms of his composition and present them to the library, the institution considering this a valid publication. While institutions have accepted this legal fiction with much grace, they have steadfastly refused to compromise the question of a size of margin on the paper or the neatness of the typed copy. A literature has grown up specifying in detail the format of these compositions. The difficulty for an average student of coping with these technical questions has given impetus to the specialization of typing bureaus, which have the leisure to become acquainted with the various esoteric requirements.

In practice, any typing bureau will on occasion correct errors in punctuation or obvious barbarisms. From correcting manuscripts to rewriting them and finally to writing them *ab ovo* has been an inevitable progression. In addition, the typing bureaus have served as a natural meeting place for rational students and artisans, contributing greatly to the professionalization of the occupation of thesis writing.

The techniques that we have discussed by no means exhaust the possibilities. Considerations of space prevent a more complete examination. But it is necessary to make some reference to the techniques of an area not heretofore discussed.

Diplomas are awarded for a series of units that are roughly equivalent to semester hours. Requirements vary from institution to institution, but the average number of undergraduate units is about 128. These are taken in subbargains, a block of 2, 3, or 4 being considered a course. Subbargains are bound to vary in the difficulty they present to students, who must meet some varying requirements to achieve the units. In theory, courses that involve greater time and effort on the part of the student receive a higher unit rating, that is to say, difficulty per unit should be equivalent. In practice, very little is done to maintain this standard. Since units are indivisible, finer distinctions cannot be made. Therefore, a wide range of difficulty per unit is available. The number of units per subbargain is set by the university and is not, like price, adjustable to the effect of supply and demand. We may expect that rationality would dictate that the courses having the lowest difficulty per unit would tend to be selected. Several factors, however, mitigate this tendency.

First, the institution requires that its blocks of units be collected from mutually exclusive subbargains. Even the course with the lowest difficulty per unit can therefore be taken only once by a student. Second, a certain number of specific subbargains are often required of each student, which further limits the fluidity of the market. Third, certain forms of packaged purchases, called majors, are required. Finally, entrance is limited in some cases. At times, the prerequisite for the purchase of a subbargain is the purchase of one or more other subbargains. At other times, the number of purchasers of a course in any one semester is limited. By virtue of these varying considerations, the market pressure toward equalizing the difficulty per unit is much reduced. Selection between the subbargains, therefore, is not a process of determining subtle marginal differentiations, but is a gross process of evaluation. The possible saving of time and effort by rational choice is far larger than would exist in a completely free market.

What, then, determines the choice of subbargains? The student cannot have had previous experience with the course, except in the comparatively rare situation where he has previously committed himself to its purchase but been unwilling or unable to meet the requirements. He must purchase a commodity not previously sampled. Despite this, an experienced student can make a comparatively sharp estimate of the difficulty per unit of a subbargain. Generally, he has access to various students who have in a previous semester purchased the course. Rational behavior suggests that this information be collected wherever an estimate is required. Further, the student has in many cases purchased a subbargain given by the same instructor as the course he is considering. Schoolwise students soon discover that, despite the advertising in the catalogue, the habits of the instructor offer a far better indication of the difficulty per unit than does the putative subject matter of the course. Rational students, then, are able to evaluate courses with a fair degree of accuracy and to opt those courses, technically known as crap courses, with low difficulty per unit.

For heuristic purposes, we have been considering each student as determining his own utility and choices, with such limitations as are the nature of the marketplace. Since, however, utility is in some measure a function of the groups a person participates in and the reference groups he acknowledges, it behooves us to take some notice of the formal and informal organizations on campus and to assess the general direction of the effects that these groups have on educational activity.

Education brings together large numbers of students of the same age and, to a lesser degree, of the same background and interest. Since the educational enclave itself occupies only a part, and often a small one, of the student's time and energy, he is free to engage in such social activities as opportunity and predisposition suggest. Thus, a large number of formal and informal groups arise and maintain themselves on campus. Groups tend to develop norms and to reward adherence to them and limit deviation from them.

As students are rationally motivated to maximize the prestige of their diploma, we may expect student associations to develop norms in line with this policy. The simplest and most obvious of these is a review of minimization techniques with a view to selecting those techniques most consistent with maximization. Since the value of a diploma is a function of the apparent effort of students, those minimizing techniques that do not detract from the apparent effort are more economical, all other things being equal, than those that do. Thus, minimizations that are least likely to become matters of common knowledge receive a premium value. The function of the association as a clearing-house is in this way doubly satisfying. It not only allows greater minimization, but it allows the student to minimize within the confines of the institution, where he might otherwise be forced to seek aid in minimization from those outside the institution, with the consequent risk of lowering the value of the diploma.

It is not necessary to examine each of the minimization processes discussed with a view to estimating the degree to which each contributes to or detracts from maximization. Suffice it to say that such an examination is part of the regular rational procedure of students and student associations. The general principle that the publicity of the minimizing procedure, beyond the amount necessary for its effective operation, is inversely proportional to the maximization sufficient to allow maximization to be calculated by an interested party. It should be kept in mind that in this context minimization and maximization do not have equal weight. The advantages for minimization are immediate, while those for maximization are remote and conditional. Heavy weighting must then be given to the minimization function. Thus, maximization may change the method selected for minimizing, but is unlikely to cause a student to forego a minimization completely.

Student groups differ both in the degree to which they are committed to educational goals and in the particular goals in which they are interested. The norms of a given group are closely tied to the nature of the leadership of that group. Although social psychologists have been unable to arrive at any consensus as to which came first, the norm of the group or the ideas of the leaders, we may safely assume that these are fairly consonant in any continuing group. In general, leadership is taken from those strata that enjoy special qualifications for participation in the educational process.

Some few associations follow the pattern dictated by the leadership of those with claims to intellectual prowess. These place various evidences of intellect at a premium and attempt to enhance the value of the institutional diploma by associating it with signs of intellectual effort.

More often, leadership is drawn from those students whose claims are based on prestige or championship. While these groups do not always share the same goals, they are often able to form a common front, in part because prestige groups in our society are often devoted to sport. Those students who can in themselves combine both of these claims can often enjoy a super-lative position on campus, by their example and leadership unifying the prestige and championship groups.

Associations taking their tone from such leadership are partic-ularly devoted to minimizing the time and effort required to meet institutional demands. Since the claims of these strata to participation in the education process are based on a secure foundation outside the intellectual sphere which supplies the rationale for many of the institutional requirements, such leaders have much leeway in organizing rational evasions. Associations, then, are able to set up optimum minimization as a norm. They often maintain such honorific titles as the gentleman's C for particular evidence of minimization and such denigrating sobriquets as drudge, bookworm, or grind to stigmatize those who attempt to depart from the high standards set.[1]

The goals set by these associations might well be unrealistic if the association, as such, made no attempt to implement them, but relied solely on the individual resources of its members. In order to aid less exemplary members and to raise the tone of the group generally, the association serves as a conference for the exchange and development of minimization methodologies and as a clearinghouse for technical aids to minimization. The spirit of cooperation forged in these associations makes possible larger-scale minimizations which would be impractical if dependent upon the vagaries of chance meeting. The associations, therefore, form a natural mart where potential partners in a minimization procedure may come together, with the resultant increase in scope and intensity of minimization.

Perhaps more importantly, these associations serve as the foci for procedures for the maximization of values for the diploma. While minimization can, and often is, practiced individually or in small groups, maximization of value requires the use of more organized methods. For the value of a diploma depends on the recognition it receives, that is, on the appearance it possesses of being of some value. It is in the nature of man to recognize the existence of something in which great pride is taken and to which great attention is paid. While semanticists and psychologists argue the nature of the phenomenon, student associations, like pantomimists, take advantage of it.

While student associations may have national structure, the operating unit is a single campus. Primarily, it is the value of a single institution's diploma that is being maximized. The associations foster the belief that attendance at a particular institution is a signal honor, their own institution being in some mysterious and undefined manner elevated above its fellows. The alumni of the institution, therefore, are people set apart from their fellows and, man for man, superior. In general, when a person undertakes to declare himself superior with the implication that his listener is a member of a lower order, he can expect to be viewed askance. On the other hand, when he declares his listener in on the higher status, he may expect a more favorable reception. Thus it comes about that, while students of a particular institution meet only qualified success in advancing their claims upon outsiders, they succeed in far greater measure in convincing each other.

When a student has been for a few years accustomed to the idea that his participation in the educational process in a particular institution entitles him and his schoolmates to a special distinction, it is unlikely that the effect will be entirely lost. After his education is complete, if his recognition of fellow alumni as superior is reciprocated, it will be maintained. Since it is often of great advantage in the business world to have a supply of people whose loyalty can be depended on to a greater degree than is usual, fellow alumni, like relatives, are often better suited as candidates for positions.

The effect is to some degree circular. Where the students know that graduation from a particular school offers them advantages in businesses employing fellow alumni, their sense of the value of a diploma is increased, adding a rational component to the psychological base of preference for one's own institution. The augmented opinion of the diploma, in turn, causes others to value their diploma more highly.

While all of these considerations give a value to the diploma of any institution, the value of the diploma is not without some objective criteria. These objective criteria depend on the effort that students are seen as making to the maintenance of prestige, championship, or intellect while at the institution or afterward. Since anyone making an effort is to a degree affected by the encouragement his exploits receive from those about him, the efforts of a student can be stimulated by organized approval. Which type of effort is stimulated is determined by the nature or leadership of the association. Those associations with intellectual bent encourage efforts in this direction. Those with prestige or championship tendencies attempt to mobilize the students to cheer on feats of championship. Although there is little experimental data to indicate the degree to which vigorous approval improves performance, it is generally held in student circles that widespread approval by the student body is a necessary condition for successful championship at the lists. In any event, associations glorify the exploits of their fellow students, giving maximum publicity to these claims for the educational excellence of their institution. School spirit, as this vigorous approval is called, becomes, therefore, one of the rational norms maintained by student associations.

The administration is understandably interested in maintaining the prestige of its diploma, to the point where it is unwilling to leave its maintenance to the unaided efforts of the student associations. Institutions have therefore taken to hiring coaches, faculty members whose duty it is to aid students in preparation for the lists. At one time, this function was served by faculty members with regular duties, the more conscientious institutions taking care that at least one faculty member be hired whose natural inclination would lead him to this activity. With time and increased competition, the practice became more formalized, and the pretense of lecturing was dropped. Today the coach is recognized as a full member of the faculty. If salary is taken as an indication—and it may fairly be so taken in a capitalist society—he is one of the more important members.

In fact, the coach serves several additional functions. By inclination or by specific request, he aids in organizing the maximizing efforts of the student associations. While he may, on occasion, cooperate in the minimizing effort as well, this has not as yet received formal approval from the administration.

The coach's support of student organizations is not maintained entirely as a species of altruism. The existence of vociferous student organizations, eager for victories at the lists, besides encouraging the desired victories serves to persuade the administration to spend more money on list activities, not infrequently including the coach's salary. A similar pattern of circular encouragement occurs between coach, alumni, and administration. Here the coach encourages the administration to spend money on the lists, to persuade the alumni to contribute, and persuades the alumni to contribute to encourage administrative support of list activities.

Alumni, although their educational bargain is completed, may still derive some benefits in addition to those acquired at the conclusion of their educational career. Having expended all the time and effort necessary, minimization is no longer possible. It is possible to maximize the value of the diploma. They can augment this value of discriminating in favor of their fellow alumni, vociferously approving the activities of student champions, or aiding in publicizing the institution's claims to prestige. Since all of these activities tend to reflect favorably on their instigators, their rationality is obvious. Those methods which are the results of habituation, most noticeably vociferous approval, are the most common, as mankind is ever most motivated to the rational activity that custom has hallowed.

Alumni are, of course, in a considerably different financial position from students. For the most part, they are earning their own living. Their desire to maximize the prestige of their diploma can be put to some use by the institution. The institution, therefore, in its perennial search for revenue, pays special attention to the alumni. Its appeal may be especially effective in that the alumnus who contributes is offering another the privilege of undergoing the donor's own ennobling experience. Not less important, perhaps, is the tax exemption. Whatever the reasons, alumni rank high on the institution's list of potential contributors. Experience has shown that alumni are particularly susceptible to appeals from the coach. To some extent this may be attributed either to the coach's rational dramatic ability or to his experience in exhorting entrants into the lists. More careful consideration suggests, however, that a perhaps larger share might be attributed to the alumni's wish to raise the prestige of the diploma.

7

The Institution's Fulfillment of Contract

Educational institutions are either public or private. For the most part, private enterprises are motivated by the desire for profit. Thus, for example, while a shoe factory may serve a function in the community, it decides business matters not on the basis of its function but in such a way as to maximize profit. Similarly, private educational institutions set academic policy by maximizing profit.*

While a business determines pricing policies, as it handles

---

* It is to be understood that profit and loss represent the positive and negative sides of a continuum. In any particular case, therefore, maximizing profit may be, in fact, minimizing loss. It is in this sense that the expression "maximizing profits" is used in this work.

By and large, educational institutions maximize profits. For various diplomatic reasons, however, institutions prefer to consider that they are operating at a loss. This can be accomplished rather easily by considering only half the budget, excluding contributions and prospective contributions.

other decisions, with a view to increasing revenue, the objective situation makes certain alternatives more rational. In this way, the judgments independently arrived at by various concerns follow certain patterns, predictable in theory from an analysis of the market.

The educational institution desires to maintain prestige to the degree that maintenance attracts more students and raises the income of the institution. While the institution has no prejudices against increasing the cost to the student in time, labor, or money, there is a point for each institution where an increase in cost will lower, rather than raise, the income.

The position of this optimum point determines the rational policy of the institution. Like any manufacturing concern, it is motivated to seek the production of a commodity of that value which will optimize profit. The prestige of a diploma, however, is not an absolute, but is relative to other diplomas. The institution with the most prestigious diploma has, therefore, an optimum point only slightly higher than that of its competitors. For an increase in prestige will not attract further students, the institution already attracting the group willing to pay the highest cost. Increasing cost unduly will only lower the size of the student body.

Other institutions have traditional prestige levels and will have a potential student body that anticipates enrollment on the basis of the tradition. As we have noted, any sizable increase in educational charges will make inroads into this potential. But the increase in prestige is less likely to come to the attention of other potential students who might be interested and these are likely to have less confidence in the institution's new prestige level than they will in the level of an institution with a tradition of higher prestige. Institutions seeking to increase prestige appreciably, therefore, face an initial loss of revenue. While decreases in prestige are even more attractive, rapid decreases, as has been pointed out, cause transitional difficulties.

The system has a measure of equilibrium, at least in respect to potential changes in prestige. Each institution's optimum point of prestige tends to remain close to its present level.

The complexities of education become more apparent when they are not dependent directly on the efforts of the student body, but upon the apparent efforts. For example, if a student body contributed nothing to their diplomas, but appeared to be contributing greatly, the diploma would rise in value so long as that appearance was maintained. Further, the efforts cannot be converted easily into a single medium of exchange, for some students contribute money, some prestige, some championship, and some intellectual efforts. The value of any particular diploma may depend primarily on one of these, but is to some degree dependent on all the others. It is thus feasible to maintain the present prestige by an infinite number of formulae.

The choice of the contributing factor is of major importance to the student body, for it determines what portion of the student body is to be taxed. As in the government, where the rich desire a sales tax and the poorer classes a highly graduated income tax, there is much division among the student body on what is the most theoretically pure method of improving the diploma.

The division of the value of the diploma and the utility of the student body tends to contribute to even greater stability. For increasing the tax on one of these tends to lower the tax on the others, and to compensate partially for an increase in value in that respect by a decrease in other respects.

For example, if the institution desires to increase the value of its diploma by gaining further recognition as a school requiring intellectual effort and therefore increases the intellectual requirements, it may expect that students who are prepared to pay in prestige or championship will be less likely to attend and, as a result, the institution's reputation in these areas will suffer. Similarly, an attempt to attract athletes will cost some prestigious candidates and some intellects.

The amount of movement possible is therefore governed by the group having the best bargaining position. In large measure these are the prestigious students. They have several advantages. First, all other groups pay in effort for their contribution. The champion must constantly practice to maintain his prowess for the lists. The intellect must keep abreast of the standard amounts of knowledge expected of him. The prestigious student, however, need only exist. He is in the position of a person holding a lighted candle and asked to light someone else's; the increased light does not diminish his own.

Furthermore, this group enters the institution with status. Therefore, the increment provided by the diploma is of the least utility to this group. Any additional requirement made of this group will have the greatest effect in reducing the number of candidates.

Finally, this group has a bargaining point in that the highest proportion of the total eligible prestigious candidates are enrolled. A school may hope to persuade a champion or an intellect who might otherwise remain uneducated to attend, but the competition for prestige students is feasible only be raiding the roster of candidates for other institutions. In terms of game theory we may say that in respect to the value of education acquired from statused students, institutions as a group are a zero sum game; in respect to value acquired from championship or intellect, institutions as a whole are not a zero sum game.[1]

The interest of each educational institution dictates that it make no attempt to raise the prestige of its diploma suddenly, since the immediate threat of a decrease in the size of the student body keeps the optimum prestige value close to the present value. While this state of the market renders the switch to an expensive product irrational, the same arguments do not operate in the opposite direction. The institution has the alternative of lessening the prestige of its diploma available to it. Many businesses have chosen to produce more items more cheaply as a method of increasing their share of the market, hence, their profits.

As a matter of fact, educational institutions have adopted this policy to some degree. The number of persons contracting for education has increased steadily from year to year to the point where it now includes a sizable proportion of the potential market.

There are, however, several factors that tend to limit the expansion of sales in this direction. First, the saturation of the market makes sales increasingly difficult with time. Where only

10 per cent of the population own a commodity, increasing production can be more easily absorbed than where 90 per cent possess the commodity.[2] While not all of the potential purchasers have contracted for education, something approaching saturation is within the foreseeable future. Of course, even in a saturated market, there will be some few for whom the cost does not equal the utility.

In the case of many products, it is possible to sell several items to the consumer. The manufacturers of automobiles and television sets have shown that even comparatively expensive commodities can be sold as additional items under certain circumstances. The existence of graduate schools demonstrates the same process in education.

Nevertheless, the theory of marginal utility quite reasonably points out that utility for any one individual decreases with the number of similar items possessed. We may assume, then, that there is some limit to expansion in this direction howbeit somewhat elastic.

Until the market has reached quite close to the saturation point, however, there will be some incentive for concerns to switch production to less valuable versions of their products. Of course, there are some difficulties attendant on this decision, but the history of businesses in the Western world amply proves that these obstacles can be overcome.

Educational institutions do, however, have some circumstances that distinguish them from the majority of businesses. Most businesses in Western society are characterized by the finality of bargains and by earnings derived largely, if not exclusively, from customers. In educational bargains, per contra, the graduate's purchase continues to fluctuate in value with changes in policies in the institution. A graduate of an institution that has opted to increase its student body markedly enjoys some difficulty in attempting to explain that he graduated in the days when the institution was different. As a result, graduates are motivated to varying degrees to persuade the institution to maintain the prestige of its diploma.

In the ordinary circumstances of the business world, a manufacturing concern is under little constraint to accept advice and suggestions from past customers. Educational institutions, however, receive only a small part of their revenue from student fees. The difference between income from students and expenses must be made up by donations from various sources, living, dead, and institutional. To some varying degree, alumni contribute to educational institutions. To the degree that they do, they exercise influence on the policies of the institution.

Educational institutions have, therefore, to face the possibility of increased difficulty in fund raising in addition to the more conventional business problems in attempts to invade the mass market.

These deterrents apply to rapid expansion into the mass market. Where the movement is gradual, there is little hindrance. The path to increased profits, therefore, is a slower one in education than in most businesses.

As the foregoing analysis has been made for private educational institutions as a group, it must be noted in passing that the various considerations apply differentially to different institutions. All sorts of local conditions must be taken into account to explain the policy of a single institution. As a group, however, the condition of the educational marketplace constrains a moving equilibrium so that the lowering of the prestige of the diploma and the expansion into the mass market proceed at a steady, if sedate, pace.

Public educational institutions face a somewhat different situation. Rational policy decisions require consideration of several factors absent from the calculations of private institutions.

In a democracy, political parties are elected by a majority of the votes. The policies adopted by these parties are dictated in large measure by considerations of popular appeal. There are, of course, instances where political parties have supported courses of action for other reasons, just as there are examples of business decisions attributable to motives other than profit. But a party that consistently makes decisions regardless of public support runs the risk of losing office just as the concern that makes decisions regardless of profit motives runs the risk of bankruptcy.

In the political field, then, we may consider the maximizing of votes as the equivalent of the maximizing of profit in economic theory.[3] Public educational institutions are therefore rational for political parties. The families of potential students possess votes. While the party that encourages the spread of public educational institutions cannot depend on gaining these votes, a party that opposes this policy can count on losing at least some of these votes. Public education is therefore likely to be bipartisan.

The administration of public institutions is then a political question. Appointed administrators are necessarily at least semi-political figures. Even the heads of private educational institutions, it may be noted, are not immune to political ambitions. Two of the twentieth century's ten presidents of the United States were heads of private educational institutions.

As a political figure, the president of an educational institution is rationally motivated to increase the size of the student body. In some states the public institution is legally required to accept all applicants meeting certain qualifications. Even in the absence of legal constraint, political self-interest will dictate large student bodies.

Public institutions are constrained by economic considerations, although these remain subordinate to political considerations. A larger student body entails a lower cost per student to the institution. This is an attractive selling point. While the cost to the institution for each additional student falls, the total cost to the institution does rise. The legislature will have to underwrite increasing losses. Since losses must be met by taxation or public debt, the interest of which must be paid by taxation, a large loss may threaten to reduce votes. Several factors combine to weaken the threat, however. First, taxes are not distributed equally among voters, but are concentrated. Benefiting many at the expense of a few is a rational political policy in a democracy, provided that the benefits are more salient to the gainers than the losses to the losers. Second, in a situation in which election depends on a passionate majority, the education of a child is likely to be more visible than an increase in taxes, the more so as the increase cannot easily be traced to any specific governmental outlay. Third, it is possible by astute budgeting to conceal deficits, passing much of the taxation burden onto future generations, whose voters are impotent to affect the careers of those responsible.

Public institutions can no more afford to devaluate the diploma completely than can private institutions. Potential students of a public institution are free to accept or reject the educational bargain. While the State may, for political purposes, pay the tuition, education is still not free. The student must suffer some immediate loss by removal from the labor force, as well as expenditure of some time and energy as his share of the bargain. If the prestige of the diploma decreases, there will be some number of students who will fail to opt the bargain. Some of these may choose a private education, others no education. In either event, there may be political repercussions. Further, the alumni of public institutions possess votes which may be used to good effect to indicate their displeasure at the economic loss involved in the devaluation of their diploma.

A marked increase in the prestige which requires additional cost to the students in time and effort may lead the institution to a similar result. The families of potential students interested in minimizing the expenditure of time and effort represent a sizable bloc of votes which must be courted.

The optimum point for the prestige of the diploma, like its private counterpart, tends, then, to remain in equilibrium. While the long-range considerations demand expansion up to the saturation point of the market, short-range considerations demand a gradual approach. We see that a set of circumstances different from those facing private institutions constrains public educational institutions to move in the same general direction.

In theory, the aims of an institution are as clear-cut as those of a student. In practice, the situation is more complicated. Where students carry out their own actions, institutions must depend on the efforts of administrators to serve their purposes. Since the administrators have ends of their own to serve, as well as institutional goals, the possibility of conflict of interest is present. Of course, over long periods, an administrator must, to some degree, carry out the aims of the institution if he is to remain employed. His own interests, therefore, can be conceptualized as modifying to some degree his official actions. We will, therefore, have to consider not only what is rational for an institution, but also what is rational for the administration of that institution, the degree to which there is overlap, and the freedom the administration has to advance its own interests when there is a divergency.

In general, while the administration is highly motivated to maintain the appearance of maximizing profit, any particular administrator is interested in minimizing only that cost that does not directly or indirectly contribute to his own profit or prestige. It is an accepted dictum of management that the person who supervises fifty people expects to be paid, and is paid, *ceteris paribus,* more than the supervisor of twenty people.[4] Thus, every department head is rationally motivated to reduce the operating costs of all other departments, while expanding his own. Tactically, however, it may be necessary to form alliances with other department heads, supporting their claims for increased budgets in return for their support of one's own. We may leave the finer details of these political transactions to the strategic experts, confining ourselves to the observation that the rise of an administration entails a certain amount of cost which follows from the self-interest of the administrators.

While the self-interest of members of the administration on the lower rungs of power is necessarily limited, chiefly by lack of opportunity, the administrator on a high level finds little minimization of cost which is not in conflict with his own self-interest. Nevertheless, his responsibility and accountability to the institution requires that he present a record of maximum profit. He will, therefore, prefer to maximize his profit by the increase of revenue rather than the decrease of expenses, a proceeding that can simultaneously satisfy the institution and himself. Keeping in mind, then, the various motivations of institutions and administrations, let us consider some of the procedures by which institutions seek to implement their objectives.

For several hundred years, the primary source for minimizing cost has been mass production.[5] This has allowed for cost reduction by means of specialization and increased use of plant. Where businessmen or economists have spoken of mass production, however, they have done so with a number of implicit assumptions, only some of which are applicable to the educational scene. In producing pins, for example, specialization will allow a worker to produce a pin in considerably less time than he otherwise could. It is assumed that this extra time will accrue to the owners of the factory.

In education, such a situation is difficult to achieve. However much an institution might like to educate a student in two years rather than four, it cannot. Pin manufacturers have been able to depend on the fact that a pin produced gives no evidence of the speed with which its manufacture has been accomplished, any pin, for all practical purposes, being equivalent to any other pin. Education, however, is largely intangible and is measured not pragmatically but historically. The amount of exposure to educational institutions is, in fact, the measure of education. The use of specialization to reduce the total time of manufacture per education per student is therefore impossible.

This does not mean that mass production is debarred. Other forms are possible. For example, increasing the size of classes, while it does not decrease the time of manufacture for any one student, does decrease the cost per item produced for the institution. It is, therefore, from the point of view of the institution, a positive good, much to be sought. It will be kept in mind that this does not involve any specialization; the professor is doing exactly the same amount and kind of work in addressing fifty students as in addresssing ten.

Three factors limit the speed of increase of size of class. First, the demand for education at any one time is, within certain limits, a constant. Although the lowering of cost to the student or the increasing of the value of the diploma may attract a certain number of persons otherwise likely to have considered and rejected the possibility of education, the number of persons in this category is comparatively small. Also, few people consider buying more than one education. Institutions operate in a market that is, therefore, highly saturated. Nor can they count on the collapse of their competitors. Institutions, like railroads, and unlike pin manufacturers, are assumed to be semipublic utilities. Years or even decades of operation at a loss do not serve to close any large number. For any one institution, the number of students enrolled sets an upper limit to the size of class.

Second, the construction of the university's plant presents an upper limit. If an institution has classrooms that seat fifty students, it can enroll perhaps one hundred students for any particular course, counting on the students' minimizing procedure to prevent overcrowding. But it would be inadvisable in the present state of student rationality to exceed this limit. While it is theoretically possible for an institution to attempt a program of increasing the students' rationality, which would allow a plant to handle increased numbers of students at the same time, such a program is, by present standards of public acceptance, likely to reflect on the institution's diploma. As we have seen, the institution is under some constraint to maintain a certain value for its diploma, at least to the degree that overt public actions that reflect on its value must be eschewed. Tacit acceptance by the institution of such minimizing procedures as students have arrived at independently of the institution are not generally felt to menace the diploma and may be safely exercised by the institution in its program to minimize expenses.

In general, the older the plant, the more likely an institution is to be handicapped in its minimization. Architects, like road builders, have almost invariably underestimated future traffic. Nor do present architects seem less conservative. Generally, institutional buildings are constructed to handle the traffic that may reasonably be expected within the next decade or two, rather than within the next century. Although this may seem at first blush an irrationality, a little consideration will show that construction of larger classrooms will require a larger immediate outlay. The ultimate economy resulting from larger classrooms will not be apparent for perhaps twenty or thirty years, beyond the expected reign of the present administrators. To expect the present generation to spend money for the benefit of future successors is not a demand made seriously of any other group of men.

Finally, there are some institutions which, in the process of selling prestige diplomas, attempt to capitalize on the lack of impersonality of instruction. They maintain a class size sufficiently smaller than the norm to allow marginal differentiations. At present, an institution in this category boasts of a class size of thirty rather than fifty. In large measure, these institutions are the ones with older plants, who are seeking to make an advantage of necessity, passing the loss due to inability to mass produce onto the consumers in the increased cost of education.

Although the time from the entrance of the student to his exit, diploma in hand, is fixed by public expectations of the value of the diploma, the amount of exposure of the student during those four years is not similarly defined. The institution has some discretion concerning the length of the academic year, subject to such decisions of the State Legislature as apply. A reduction in the number of days per semester represents a largely indirect saving for the institution. It will be noted, for example, that American high schools have a 180-day year, while their Dutch counterparts have a school year of 240 days, each day being 10 per cent longer.

The institution directly saves the cost of heating the plant on days when there are no classes, a minor but helpful saving. Further, the effort for students is reduced, which allows some increase in the number of students. More important, however, the long summer vacation allows teachers to hold summer jobs. This possibility reduces greatly the pressure to increase salaries, which represent a major cost item in the institutional budget.

It is a maxim of economics that the increased use of plant reduces the cost per unit produced, since the fixed charges that the plant represents can be distributed among more units. The amount of expense minimizing that is possible through this procedure depends to some degree on the size of the plant relative to the number of students. When the plant is of more than adequate size, scheduling classes at earlier and later hours does not provide a saving, but requires additional heating, or a loss.

Where the plant is relatively small, adroit scheduling accommodates more students, which would otherwise be impossible without further building.

There is some limit to the degree to which this procedure can be followed. Where use of the elective system permits, students avoid classes at hours they find inconvenient, even on occasion accepting a class with a greater difficulty per unit credit for the sake of a desirable schedule. Scheduling at odd hours is, therefore, to some degree limited to required courses. Even here, the inconvenience to the student cannot be increased to the point where it is a source of public complaint, which might restrict the number of future students. Still further, not all rooms are interchangeable. Certain laboratories, gymnasiums, and music rooms can be used only for particular classes. Maximization procedures for these must be separately calculated and are worth introducing, like the maximizing for undifferentiated schoolrooms, only where the facilities are relatively inadequate.

The limitations on increased use of plants hold only in regard to the students regularly enrolled. Where additional students can be enrolled who will make use of the plants during what would otherwise be off-hours, a marked minimization of expense is possible. Thus, institutions are motivated to start programs for persons employed during the daytime and for adult education courses. The latter are particularly helpful to the institution in the cases where a diploma is not granted. In such cases, procedures for minimizing expenses may be employed that would otherwise be inadmissible because of the possible lowering of the value of the prestige token.

Mass production in the field of education has been described as consisting of increasing the size of the student body, decreasing the hours of exposure per student, and increasing the use of plant. The peculiar nature of education would appear to make specialization irrational, as we have said. Yet even a glance at the catalogue of any institution reveals that specialization runs riot. It is only in the smallest of institutions that the same professor teaches English and history. The institution no sooner gets big enough for two professors in this position than it boasts a history professor and an English professor, each of whom is expected to maintain at least token ignorance of the other's field. Where an institution hires two professors of English, each is expected to specialize in a different century. In fine, specialization is always pushed to the maximum point possible within the limits of the requirements set by the administration.

At first blush this specialization seems analogous to the specialization practiced in the manufacture of tangibles, where each operation is subdivided to the farthest extent allowed by the demand. But the similarity is misleading. For manufacturers of tangibles are able to hire their workers either by the piece, in which case specialization reduces total labor costs, or by the hour, in which case the increased production lowers the cost per unit. In either event, the lower cost per unit represents a direct profit to the manufacturer. This profit may be partly or completely passed on to the consumer in order to increase sales. Naturally, increased sales allow for further specialization.

In education, it is necessary to consider three different hours per student: the hour of exposure of student and professor, the hour spent by the student meeting institutional requirements, and the hour spent by the faculty preparing for the hour of exposure. Each of these is independent of the other, an increase in one leading to no necessary increase or decrease in another.

The hours of exposure, as we have seen, are relatively fixed by fiat of State Legislature. They are, in any event, not affected by specialization.

The hours spent by the faculty in preparation are, to a degree, reduced by specialization. The time saved by specialization does not accrue to the institution, since the hours of exposure per faculty member are fixed by custom and agreement, which would not allow the institution to add to the teaching load, as the hours per professor are entitled, the amount saved by specialization. In any event, the amount saved is not great, since preparation time is minimal after the first five or so years of teaching when the routine has been more or less committed to memory and can be recalled by a rapid glance at previously prepared notes during the first few minutes of an exposure hour.

Specialization is much favored by faculty, for other reasons as well. It presents a professor with two advantages. First, it greatly increases marginal differentiation, a definite asset to a professor changing positions. Second, it reduces overt competition between professors at the same institution. As we will see later, academic life is highly competitive to a degree where any device to depersonalize and mask competition is a premium. Where, for example, rivalry between two English professors might be seen as resulting from competitiveness, acquisitiveness, animosity, or pique, as a result of specialization it may be viewed as a difference of opinion on the relative utility or aesthetic value of Chaucer as compared to Pope. Thus, the timid may see specialization as a defense against the pressure of colleagues, while the aggressive may see it as a mask for sharper attacks on others.

In any event, the specialized institution has an advantage in attracting faculty, which is, on occasion, a convenience.

For the student, specialization does decrease somewhat the time and effort needed to meet institutional demands. For specialization increases the range of difficulty per unit of the various courses. As a result, it is easier for the rational student to select those courses with the least difficulty per unit.

The chief advantage, however, that specialized institutions have in regard to students is the marginal differentiation they enjoy. Where the candidate is offered so large a range of possible partners to his education, marginal differentiation is a marked boon to institutions so advantaged. Specialization then results in attractiveness to students.

While attractiveness to students and faculty is a competitive advantage to the institutions that enjoy it, it does not contribute to the total amount of education bought. Specialization may persuade a candidate to prefer one institution over another; it will not persuade him to become educated.

Since the institutions are highly competitive, however, the adoption of specialization by any one of them forces the others to specialize in order to retain their share of the market. For, as we have seen, the price of a smaller student body is a higher cost per student, fixed charges not being reduced with the reduction in the student body. Specialization tends, then, to proceed to the limit allowed by the distribution of students in the different institutions.

While all institutions are compelled to specialize to the degree that the size of the student body permits, specialization does not leave unaltered the relative size of student bodies. For the larger institutions are capable of more specialization. Hence, the effect of specialization is to increase the enrollment of large universities at the expense of small ones.

Several factors act to inhibit this tendency. First, some institutions are prevented from markedly increasing their student body by the size of their plant. Second, many large institutions enjoy low prestige, which even a high degree of specialization does not offset. Finally, institutions incapable of a high degree of specialization make a virtue of necessity, calling the lack of specialization a basic curriculum, much in the fashion that institutions with an obsolete plant advertise the personal nature of the teaching system.

The rise of specialization has required the use of the elective system, it being impossible for a student to take every subbargain offered. As we have seen, the rational students will minimize effort by opting courses with a low difficulty per unit. The effect of rationality, therefore, produces a Gresham's Law of education: courses with a low difficulty per unit will drive courses with a high difficulty per unit out of circulation. This law, however, does not operate with the elegance of its monetary counterpart. For courses are given by professors who do not take the disinterested attitude adopted by gold coins toward retirement from the marketplace. Instead, professors vie with one another for the favor of student enrollment in their courses. To some degree, an appeal to the rationality of the students is adopted. Reduction of the difficulty per unit, where suitably publicized, will provide incentive for increased enrollment in any particular course, to the detriment of alternative courses.

Such a policy is not without its dangers. The attractiveness of the subbargain is not a simple inverse function of its absolute difficulty per unit, but depends on the relative difficulty per unit.

In a market without forced purchases or tie-in sales, each student purchases as many subbargains as are required, selecting them by the principle of least difficulty per unit. A subbargain's position in the hierarchy is, therefore, dependent not only on the difficulty per unit encountered, but on the difficulty per unit of all the other subbargains offered, much as the appeal of any commodity varies according to the price of competitive products. Thus, the possibility of a price war is inherent in any sharp drop in the difficulty per unit of a particular subbargain.

Further, the danger of a price war is somewhat greater in educational bargains than in most economic transactions. In ordinary business dealings, the cost per unit to the seller is likely to provide a floor beneath which prices cannot safely fall. While a single concern can sell below its cost for a short time in order to drive its competition from the marketplace, this is at best a temporary expedient, since all are dependent on profit to survive. The faculty member is not in this sense dependent on the difficulty per unit. If all the faculty were to join in the competitive reduction in difficulty, their livings would not thereby be imperiled. There is some long-range danger of menacing the prestige of the diploma, but this is by no means of the same order of magnitude as the danger of lack of profit is to a businessman. The danger may, in fact, never materialize.

If all faculty members reduce the difficulty per unit to the point where it is negligible, however, the attendance in any specific course will tend to randomness. Those faculty members who now possess a share of the trade of the student body larger than their expected random proportion are, then, motivated to avoid price wars. The exact number that would constitute a random share is rarely calculated, so that professors are often free to give themselves the benefit of the doubt in the matter. There is, therefore, some pressure upon faculty members to resist the drives of the marketplace.

These tendencies are strengthend by the existence of alternative methods of raising the attractiveness of the subbargain. Professors may choose an irrational appeal. Paradoxical as this may seem, the rationality of irrational appeals is common not only in education but also in business and politics. The professor is therefore motivated to turn entertainer, regaling his students with gossip, patter, and numerous anecdotes. Practitioners of such an art are to some extent limited to those who have some talent for these productions, these being able to feel safe from retaliation from less gifted colleagues. The criterion for entering this particular form of academic competition, however, is not the existence of talent but the psychological confidence that talent exists, which may well occur in the absence of talent. Since students may be as much amused by observing the efforts of an untalented but zealous performer as by the smoother productions of a master, the attendance at courses given by entertainers will not necessarily disillusion the untalented. The ability of the faculty to appeal to the irrationality of the student allows the benefits of specialization to be spread more evenly among the faculty. For the marginal differentiation afforded would be counterbalanced to a large extent for any professor if the price were failure to enroll students in his own course. While the faculty, as we shall see, have their own standards for evaluating performances, the administration much prefers to hire a professor who can attract students. Although faculty satisfaction is not a necessity for the institution, it is conducive to the ease with which the administration can deal with the faculty it employs.

Specialization, as we have seen, does not increase the productivity of the faculty markedly. Institutions have begun exploring another approach; automation. From a technical standpoint, it is presently possible to replace the faculty with a series of robots, for the purposes of lecturing, at least. Films, kinescopes, and television will present the student with an audiovisual experience not markedly different from a more conventional lecture.

The substitution of automatic professors has proceeded only slowly, however, despite the obvious saving in expense. Several considerations have dictated caution. The initial expense of automation has been high. Of course, this inhibition is only temporary. Automation of any sort has tended to be expensive. Yet it has rarely failed to occur for that reason. Education, however, has some unusual problems. It is of the essence of the bargain that prestige be conferred. While a robot professor may say the same words and make the same gestures as the original, it is not yet certain that he will confer the same prestige. This is, of course, a matter to be determined empirically. Until this generation, the problem has not been possible. There seems to be no theoretical reason why the public cannot be acclimated to accept faculty surrogates as valid legitimators of prestige. It may, however, take some time. Until institutions can be sure that robot professors will be acknowledged as acceptable surrogates, automation will be held up.

Public acceptance of robot instruction harbors a potential danger, however. It is important to the position of the institution that surrogates be accepted as alternative forms of faculty's presence rather than as audiovisual aids to instruction. In the latter case, the public will have absorbed the idea that instruction in the absence of the faculty is educational. This opens up the serious possibility of bootleg education. The possibility of uninvited guests at robot instruction does not constitute a menace. The techniques of movie houses and closed-circuit television are sufficiently developed to handle interlopers. The danger, of course, is in the use of a cheap audiovisual aid presently available to the public: books. Since the rise of the medieval universities, books have not enjoyed the prestige of being considered educational in the absence of professors, although they have been acceptable as supplementary educational tools. Were the robot professors to be considered as educational tools rather than as surrogate people and accepted as such, there is much risk of the distinctive nature of education being lost.

Since institutions have rationally been chary of automation of professorial duties, they might have been expected to face a steadily increasing pressure from their employees to raise wages. But this is so only under the assumption of the existence of a single labor market. Where there are no enclaves, or automomous labor markets, wages are uniform. For if one factory raises wages, workers in other factories are attracted and other factories are forced to match the raise to retain their best workers. A factory attempting to lower wages is threatened by the loss of its workers. Thus, wages remain in equilibrium throughout the system.

In fact, this elegant scheme is disrupted by the division of the market into enclaves. If a part of the market is confined to an enclave, it is surrounded by a barrier or membrane such that access to the enclave and exit from it is prohibited; the wages in the enclave are determined by conditions of supply and demand within the enclave. Wages may then maintain a separate equilibrium above or below the wage scale prevailing in the outside labor market.[6]

Membranes, however, may be unidirectional. If access to an enclave is restricted by the necessity for long and arduous training or possession of a special skill, the wages in the enclave may find an equilibrium above the prevailing wage scale. For employers in the general market will not be compelled to raise their scales to keep their workers, who are not allowed access to the enclave.

Conversely, if the membrane restricts exit, either because of the unwillingness of the worker in the enclave to leave or because of the unwillingness of the employers outside the enclave to hire workers from the enclave, the wage scale may continue below the prevailing wage scale. Employers within the enclave then will be under no necessity to raise wages to prevent the loss of workers, the membrane acting in lieu of a wage increase.

The academic enclave is to a degree restricted in both directions. Institutions require educational qualifications of their professors for a number of reasons. We find, in general, that wherever a skill is necessary in the performance of a job, that skill presents a barrier to entrance and to raise the wages for that job above the prevailing wage for unskilled labor. Where a job requires little or no skill, as in the present case, wages depend on the general labor market situation, in the absence of two conditions. To the degree that the job holders are able to organize to restrict entrance, a higher wage scale can be maintained. In general, then, the less skilled the job, the greater the rational motive for organization. In a culture where the use of naked force, except in international relations, is to a degree frowned upon, it is convenient, even where not absolutely necessary, to create a myth concerning the degree of skill required. While the organization of faculties has not proceeded to a degree of strength comparable to, say, the typographical union, they are able to exert some pressure to maintain barriers to entrance.

The chief barriers to entrance, however, arise from a second condition. Where the product is an intangible such that the purchaser cannot evaluate the product other than by confidence in the manufacturer, qualifications for the workers are required in order to maintain the prestige of the product. This is, in large measure, the case in education. It is difficult to evaluate the quality of education the graduate has received; there are far too many educational institutions to remember the standings of any but a few. Further, conditions and policies change to the degree that relative standings are not entirely stable. While the possession by the faculty of certifications of certain qualifications does not guarantee prestige, its absence is likely to lead to questions. Institutions are therefore rationally motivated to cooperate in restricting entrance. The cooperation is only partial, however. It is the appearance of cooperation rather than the cooperation itself which the need for prestige constrains. To the degree that the institution can hire faculty members lacking the prerequisites which the faculty consider necessary without the proceedings becoming a matter of public repute, it can economize. The degree to which this alternative is opted will vary with local conditions. But it serves only to qualify the general difficulty of entrance into the field.

Exit from the field may be still more difficult. To some degree, the very qualifications for entrance tend to restrict exit. Long educational preparation is an investment that will be largely wiped out by employment outside the academic world. Still more serious, however, is the unwillingness of employers to hire professors. This is a differential unwillingness, applying to some parts of the faculty much more than to others. Where the professor of Greek may find employment ouside the enclave impossible, the economist or physicist may not. Generally, the state of the market for a particular specialty is known to the practitioners of that specialty. It remains fairly constant over a short period.

The knowledge of the state of the market is similarly available to the administration. Negotiations concerning faculty salaries occurring periodically, the salary for a particular faculty member is likely to be a function of the relative bargaining skills and positions of the member and of the administration. Where the member can easily find a position outside the institution in the event that an agreement is not reached, his bargaining position is comparatively increased. Over a period of years, then, the relative salaries of different specialties will come to resemble the relative availability of outside positions for members of these specialties.

Most important, however, is the unwillingness of the academician to leave, even for a higher salary. This reflects two causes. First, as we have noted, the conditions of employment for faculty members are considerably less onerous than in most other industries. It would, therefore, take a considerable increase in salary for an outside job to pay the faculty member the same wages per hour that he now enjoys. Second, the faculty member, as part of a group that confers prestige, is automatically accorded recognition as having sufficient prestige so that contact with him confers prestige. To an extent, then, faculty members can be seen as maximizing not profit, but prestige. To the degree that prestige is independent of salary, it will be possible for wage scales in the enclave to fall below the prevailing scale in the market without necessarily reducing the supply of professors. It is the difference in utilities between the faculty and the institution that enables the wage scale of the faculty to remain low inside the enclave.

A consideration of academic tenure will serve to clarify the difference in viewpoints of the parties. Certain professorial positions are assumed to possess tenure. According to standard academic lore, possessors of tenure cannot be dismissed without just cause. Just cause is a medieval concept which, like fair price, has steadfastly defied definition and evaded substantial agreement. Notwithstanding, tenure is highly prized and sets its holder off from the lower ranks who do not possess this insignia. In fact, an administration desiring to fire a professor is almost invariably able to do so regardless of his tenure status. For the administration possesses a large number of perquisites which conduce to the pleasantness of academic life. It schedules classes, for example. It provides offices, secretarial help on occasion, raises in salary, permission for outside employment, honorific opportunities to serve on committees, and a host of other dispensations, each perhaps small in itself, but imposing in aggregate. These, together with some ability on the part of the institution to make placement at other institutions difficult or easy, gives the institution a superordinate position that no unilateral guarantee will make unreal. The institution, therefore, having no fear of tenure, can use it as a bargaining counter, like titles in lieu of salary increases.

To this point we have considered various methods institutions may employ to minimize expenditure. Every institution, however, is handicapped in its ability to minimize expenditure by the necessity of working through persons whose self-interest requires maximizing at least some expenditure. This conflict of interests gives a differential effectiveness to various methods. Any method that involves a bid for a larger student body will be supported by the administration. For a larger student body is assumed to require a larger administration, which in turn allows the upper echelon to demand higher salaries. In addition, use of the elective system adds greatly to the complexity of bookkeeping, which increases staff, also. Reduced expenditure for faculty is only partially supported by the administrators. In general, the middle echelon of business will support higher salaries for their subordinates where their own salaries are only slightly higher than their subordinate's, since any increase in the salary given to subordinates will be duplicated in their own. Where, however, there is a large discrepancy between the salaries of subordinates and superordinates, the case in education, the preferred method of raising one's own salary is to hire more subordinates. Notwithstanding, increase of demand in a limited market does have a tendency to raise salaries. The general attitude of administrators toward salary increases will, then, in large measure, depend on the facility for raising institutional income.

The ease of access to income depends on whether the institution is public or private. In a public institution, access is comparatively easy. Legislators support institutions with a generosity that is possible only to those who spend other people's income. Each additional professor or administrator hired is a political asset. The balancing political liabilities, as we have seen, are widely distributed and far less noticeable.

The problem of raising funds for a private institution is more complex. Despite heroic attempts at use of mass production methods, the relatively high labor costs of education have prevented institutions by and large from profitably selling large-scale education to lower income groups. However, educators enjoy a certain advantage that the producers of other prestige items do not: philanthropists are willing to contribute to the spread of this luxury among the population. The reasons why a philanthropist prefers to distribute diplomas among his less fortunate brethren, where he would hesitate to contribute automobiles, is a matter for the psychologist to examine; for our purposes we may take the fact for granted.

In any event, private institutions have not been slow to take advantage of the situation. It has been some centuries since the discovery that universities could have names, other than the city or province in which they are located or the purpose for which they were supposed to be established. The name was bestowed upon someone considered to be worthy of the honor. While in earlier days general service to the community or the field of education was likely to reap the prize, the field has been invaded by those whose claims to distinction rest largely on surplus resources. The comparative rarity of founding a new institution has prevented the informal procedure from acquiring a standard market price.

Over time, the institutions have explored other areas. Buildings, gymnasiums, laboratories, and even rooms have been recognized to have a marketable title. Similarly, the payment of the salary of a single professor is likely to be requited with a title, so that the professor is no longer considered the classics department but the occupant of the John Wilkes Booth Chair of Applied Latin.

To a marked degree, the extension of this new market has

been aided by the tax structure. The complicated legal status of monies is too intricate a subject to be ventured into at this point. Suffice it to say that there are instances in which the dispersal of monies to such groups as find favor in the legislators' eyes can be extremely profitable.

In course of time, the dipersal of monies, at first haphazard and ad hoc, became formalized, at least for the larger contributors, into foundations. At first these tended to make large grants to a few institutions, but they have, for policy reasons still obscure, shifted to distributing small sums to many institutions. Their criteria for selection are various, complicated, and not infrequently arbitrary. It being to the rational interests of an institution to garner as many of these grants as possible, certain administrators have been selected by the larger institutions to specialize in analyses of the criteria.

In general, the results have been in the nature of a form of diversification for the private institution. Where they would, at one time, produce only education, they now often produce various honorific recognitions for contributors and various short-term research projects for foundations. While a comprehensive study of educational practices would include a thoroughgoing analysis of the market for these prestigious by-products, the scope of this study is too sketchy to permit of such a digression. From an economic point of view, these extracurricular activities have reached such proportions that large parts of the endeavor of educational institutions are devoted to them, but at this point they are still dependent on the prestige of the institution, to the examination of which we shall now turn.

All educational institutions require the maintenance of a degree of prestige. Let us consider some of the methodologies of education in the light of this requirement.

The mainstay of educational methodology is the lecture system. This requires the mutual exposure of a professor and a large number of students for a fixed span of time, one or more times during the week. It is the accepted practice during most of this period for the professor to read aloud or speak. He may, on occasion, permit himself to be asked questions, but extended comments by students are considered inappropriate for lectures, being reserved for tutorial seminars. Although the professor may quiz the class orally, testing is usually done in writing.

A lecture is considered, by standard educational theory, to be a method of conveying information from instructor to student. Consideration of the circumstances tends to cast some doubt on the adequacy of this explanation. In most cases, the information that is purported to be conveyed has previously been printed. In those cases where unpublished information is given, the instructor is often in the process of preparing a book embodying this information, which might be speeded up if he were free to devote the lecture time to writing.

Barring unusual circumstances, then, students have access to published material containing the information read by the lecturer. Reading aloud is a somewhat time-consuming operation. A rudimentary acquaintance with the art of reading, such as is enjoyed by college students, is more than adequate to collection of information more rapidly by reading than by listening. Further, the fact that there are many students listening to a reading that can proceed only at one speed means that some students will find the rate too slow or too fast. Reading, on the contrary, is a solitary sport. Where a passage presents difficulties, it may be reread until it becomes clear. Each student may set his own pace, the reward for rapid understanding being a diminution of the time necessary to devote to the amassing of information.

Unlike the seminar, where the participation of the student may change the subject under discussion, a course of lectures is expected to follow a fixed program. In terms of information conveyed or even of convenience, then, the lecture cannot compete with the use of publications. In fact, it is in most instances a slow reading of the publication on which it is based.

Although this conclusion is patent to even the slightest consideration, it is far less generally recognized than might be imagined, due to the fact that lecturers are *pro forma* expected to speak from typed notes or from manuscripts. Of course, the custom is not the simple archaism that it might seem. It is, in fact, designed to give the impression that the information transmitted is not available in public form.

Instructors often read from preliminary drafts of their textbooks, which are to hand for this purpose. Presumably the preliminary draft is considered by the author to be less adequate than the final product. Nonetheless, the more prestigious nature of typewritten or manuscript material more than offsets the informational inferiority. In large measure, the instructor can proceed in this fashion with only the barest minimum possibility of detection, since the probability that the students will have recourse to the text is minimal. As was indicated in the previous chapter, students have access to many more rational sources of information.

It would seem, then, more realistic to consider the lecture system as a means of transferring prestige by association. A number of situations that would pose problems to the informational theory of lecturing can be understood in this framework. For example, many professors are prone to speak in a low voice, mumble, slur words, or generally maximize what is referred to in communication analysis as noise. It is rare that the lecture is audible in the rear of the room, a condition which is as ubiquitous as it is unnoticed. If we can assume that it is of the essence only that the lecture take place, not that it be heard, the situation is no longer an anomaly.

Similarly, observation indicates that classrooms are filled from the rear, wherever seats are not assigned. The front rows are commonly reserved for the tardy. Standard educational theory gives no explanation for this phenomenon. If lectures can be thought of as prestige transfers, however, the fulfillment of the contractual obligation of attendance with a minimum of effort becomes perfectly rational.

It is obvious that students with even a slight degree of sophistication operate under the tacit assumption of the prestige transfer theory. The rational student minimizes the expenditure of time and effort involved in his contractual obligation whenever possible. Avoidance of attendance entirely is obviously the greatest saving. Where attendance is checked and abstention punished, rational behavior dictates that attendance be the minimum required by rule. In practice, those classrooms where attendance is taken at the beginning of the exposure period suffer a progressive decline in the number of students with the duration of the period. Those classrooms where attendance is taken at the end of the exposure period show an analogous increase. Where roll call is the standard procedure a survey of the attendance book shows a total of attendance above that which a head count would reveal. The exact increment varies, but caution usually restricts it to about 10 per cent.

It will be seen that the maximum use of plant, a rational means of rationalizing profit for the institution, makes it necessary that the institution cooperate in the minimization techniques adopted by the students. The necessity to maintain prestige requires that the institution appear not only to oppose but also to check minimization by students. The two requirements, however, do not conflict. They only make it necessary that the institution pursue one policy while appearing to pursue another.

An institution that builds classrooms too large to allow a lecture to be heard in all parts of a room or uses classrooms that cannot seat all of the students enrolled can proceed in this rational fashion so long as no official complaints are made. While any large number of complaints would menace prestige, from whence are such complaints to come? Rational students seek only minimization. Student adherents of standard educational theory or such irrational students as the culture may periodically foster are perfectly free to attend as many lectures as they desire seated right in front of the professor, a position which few will dispute. They have no cause for complaint. The system, then, is stable.

The lecture provides both faculty and students opportunities for minimizing effort and it provides the institution the opportunity for maximizing profit.

This is, of course, the chief advantage of lecturing. There are some minor benefits. Lecturing does allow the instructor to make rational appeals to the irrational, as we have seen, by attempting to make its presentation interesting. The advantage of such behavior has already been noted and need not be repeated.

A situation somewhat analogous to the lecture situation has developed in regard to textbooks. While the standard educational theory that lectures transmit the information the course is devoted to, if it were realistic, would obviate the need for textbooks, they are, in fact, required by institutional fiat.

Textbooks are, in the main, large, bulky, cumbersome volumes printed on thick stock, replete with a plethora of illustrations, and extravagantly expensive. Outside the educational field, books have become smaller, more convenient, lighter, and cheaper. Whatever laws govern the design of books in the general marketplace would seem to have been repealed in the case of textbooks. Let us examine this paradox.

We have previously concluded from our examination of rational student behavior that the use of texts by the student for data gathering was uneconomical. This may provide a first clue to the differences between the textbook market and the general book market. Whatever considerations determine the purchase of a text, it is comparatively unlikely that it will be read. For large parts of the book market, at least, this cannot be assumed. Book reading carries prestige only in the most limited of circles, and, even in these, certain kinds of books, for example, mystery stories, westerns, modern romance novels, give little status. Whatever the final result of a purchase, therefore, books in the general market must be designed with the possibility of their being read in mind.

Textbooks, however, are purchased for display purposes. The institution requires their use as a symbol of the time, effort, and expense of acquiring an education. Few sights impress outsiders with the benefits of a college education as the appearance of a student struggling to control half a dozen thick and obviously heavy textbooks slithering in every direction on a crowded subway. A watching diplomat gives a half-smile of sympathy tempered with quiet satisfaction. A noncollege man turns his head, concealing his sudden stab of envy behind his earnest perusal of a cigarette ad. No public relations campaign could hope to match the effect.

For his part, the student makes his appearance at the institution amid a welter of texts demonstrating his earnestness. Since he has rational reason to make his appearances as infrequent as can be managed, such visits as are paid to the alma mater should make as favorable an impression on institutional personnel as possible.

In the advertising trade, it is taken as one of the more elementary principles that a display is more effective as it is larger, more colorful, and more highly illustrated. All of these aesthetic qualities, eclipsed in the general book market by more pragmatic considerations, can be given full play in textbooks.

The distinction between the requirements for text and general books is exaggerated by another consideration. Although the student buys the book, the choice of text is the professor's. The professor is, in effect, controlling the purchase of an item which he himself will not use. It is common knowledge in the general marketplace that whenever a person buys or dictates the purchase of an item for the use of another, the standard of convenience is overshadowed, if not replaced, by aesthetic considerations. A person who will buy a plainly wrapped box of chocolates for himself will spend much more for a multicolored, embossed, and beribboned box containing the same chocolates for a gift to another. Presumably new heights of artistic recognition could be reached if the recipient were to pay for the gift. But this is precisely the situation in the case of texts. The professor is free to dictate purchase according to the canons of aesthetic appeal and maximum advertising with no regard to considerations of price or convenience.

As a matter of fact, the high cost is not only a deterrent to the sale of textbooks, but it is an asset. For the laws of utility which dictate that the price is a function of utility apply to the case where the purchaser determines both the utility to himself and the price he is willing to pay. This generalization that utility determines price is sufficiently the norm that special situations tend to be viewed in the same fashion by halo effect. In the case of textbooks, the student is constrained to purchase an item, the utility of which is still unknown to him, for a price fixed by others. He then assumes the utility as proportional to the price, as a carryover from the more usual bargaining situation.

As a result, then, of the widespread tendency among students to estimate the utility of textbooks as a function of the amount they have to pay for them, it is rational for a member of the faculty to select an expensive textbook rather than a cheap one. To the degree that the textbook is considered a utility, the course that requires the textbook acquires prestige; to that degree the student is receiving his fair return in the educational bargain. Insofar as the student is paying for this utility in cash, usually his parents', rather than in time and effort, usually his own, he is unlikely to be dissatisfied with the bargain.

Two considerations do limit the tendency toward aesthetic appeal and advertising effectiveness. First, every textbook has at least one author. The author himself need not be a professor, but large numbers of them are, for reasons that will become apparent during the discussion of the nature of faculty. The author of a book regularly receives a certain payment for each copy sold. Economic considerations would indicate that the author attempt to encourage sales. A professor may easily have two hundred students in his lectures in a school year for whom he dictates the choice of texts. Over a decade he may choose texts for two thousand students. Where a book has four authors, a not unheard-of event, the writers alone may account for a sizable sale. Further, salesmen of textbooks consider that the popularity of the textbook in the field, as indicated by sales figures, is a powerful sales argument in approaching professors to encourage them to select a particular text. Assignment of a text, therefore, not only sells those texts bought by the students in the course, but encourages further assignment and purchases at other institutions. A professor, then, will be rationally motivated to select a text he has written even in preference to a heavier, glossier, and more colorful volume written by a competitor. The marketplace is to a degree hindered in its free operation by the remnants of mercantilism.

Secondly, in the course of events, periodically someone finds in a textbook a statement to which he takes exception. It is to be expected that in matters of import more than one opinion will be held in the community. It is of the nature of men that some of them are more vehement in their opinion than others. There is, therefore, scarce a viewpoint on any matter that does not have its violent partisans. Even the abandonment of violent partisanship has its violent partisans. Of course, the existence of noisy objectors poses a threat to the sales of a book. Professors, being rational people, attempt to avoid the selection of books likely to incur the wrath of the articulate. The authors, having still more at stake, take even greater pains to avoid offense. Since the discussion of a matter about which violent opinions are held cannot help but incur the displeasure of at least one side and is likely, if judiciously and temporately written, to attract the annoyance of both sides, the only safe course is to avoid the subject. The resultant productions are technically known as noncontroversial. The term is something of an exaggeration, for no book can fail to find an opponent somewhere. In any event, relatively noncontroversial texts enjoy an advantage over their more controverisal counterparts that outweigh many aesthetic advertising considerations. It is to be anticipated that, with a rising level of sophistication, it is a matter of time until all textbooks reach a standard of noncontroversiality sufficiently high that marginal differentiation will no longer be possible in this dimension and aesthetic and advertising qualities will regain their former sway.

It will be noted that the trends in the textbook market have occurred not through conscious planning or direction but, rather, by the invisible hand of the marketplace which forms a consistent pattern from the self-interest of each of the participants.

A similar pattern is seen in testing. As we have previously mentioned, the institution periodically requires that students be tested, it being universally held to be a prerequisite for the prestige of the diploma. According to standard educational theory, testing is a process of quality control which serves to screen the student body, rejecting those who are not entitled to a diploma. Several difficulties beset this theory. The general use of product control is based on the existence of a number of conditions, chief among which is that it is possible with the raw materials and the skills available to produce a product to specification with deviations limited to a fixed tolerance. Given this state, it is possible to consider the desired characteristics of the product as a given, with the processes of manufacture as variables. Periodic sampling and testing of the product will lead immediately to rejection of the unsatisfactory batch and, when rejections exceed a given rate, changes in selection of raw material, status of personnel, or method of operation.

The educational situation is not entirely analogous. The raw material is, to a large extent, given, for the institution is rationally driven to maximize the size of the student body either to gain votes or to maximize profit. But, as student bodies increase in size to the point where they account for a sizable proportion of the age group, students must become more heterogeneous. Tests, which in a former day were satisfactory, prove to reject too high a proportion to be rationally justifiable. Nevertheless, the educational system produces an intangible. No amount of measurement of tangibles will suffice to assess an education, for it is the common impression of tangible results rather than the tangible results that evaluate the education. Educational authorities, therefore, have a leeway in the modification of test procedures not usually available to industry's product control men. In view of the additional demands made upon testing by the rational necessity to use a variety of raw materials, this leeway is by no means excessive.

The foregoing analysis is a consideration of testing at an institutional level. It is necessary to consider how the autonomous action of faculty members and students leads to maximizing the utility for the institution. It must be remembered that faculty members, by and large, are no more conscious of the effects of their action in maximizing institutional utility than factory workers moving to new jobs are aware of creating an equilibrium of wages.

As part of his duties, the faculty member is required to certify or reject the title of each student in each course to having met the payments of time and effort for the units of credit which constitute the transactions which culminate in graduation. Such contact as the professor has had with the student in the course of lecturing gives no indication of the degree to which the student is able or willing to maintain the prestige of the diploma. The professor resorts to testing which yields some knowledge of the rank ordering of the students and of the absolute amounts of information available to them.

What use the professor makes of this knowledge is, of course, a matter of his own policy. He may attempt to evaluate each student independently, or he may rely instead on the rank ordering. Whatever the procedure adopted, the results over a period of time for a particular professor are likely to show a marked uniformity. While a specific class score may be lower or higher over a period of years, it will be evident that any particular professor's proportion of rejections tends to fluctuate about a constant.

Since students have invested heavily in these subbargains, they are highly motivated to seek guarantees that the institution, as represented by the professor, fulfill its share of the contract. Rational behavior would suggest that those professors who are more liberal in the use of rejections should be avoided in favor of more conservative practitioners. Since the student community over a period of time acquires comprehensive, if informal, estimates of the constants of the various professors, little expenditure of effort is required to ascertain the facts of the matter. As a result of the rational behavior of students, therefore, the proportion of an institution's students whose subbargains are negotiated with liberal professors declines; thus, the proportion of rejections to acceptances is minimized.

The number of students opting a professor, however, is of some interest to some professors. Professors are, to a marked degree, in competition with one another, and the number of students to which each lectures is taken as one index of relative standing. A professor who desires to increase the size of his classes is unaware of the effect of a more conservative attitude toward rejection. The market then tends toward an equilibrium, much in the fashion of the general labor market.

Since the forces of the marketplace tend to minimize rejection, and the rational admission policies of institutions tend to increase the heterogeneity of the student body, testing procedures require progressive adjustment. In fact, this seems to be what has happened. At one time testing was largely conducted by means of essay questions. With the increase in size of student bodies, this method has, to a marked degree, been replaced by objective testing.

Careful consideration of the nature of the different methods reveals that objective tests yield a far lower proportion of rejections, given the same initial amount and distribution of information. In a true-and-false test, for example, a purely random selection of choices leads to an average grade of 50. A grade of 70, which is in most cases a passing grade, requires an average knowledge of only 40 per cent of the bits of information tested. In most instances, multiple-choice questions show similar ratios of grade to per cent of information, since in the majority of cases a multiple-choice question presents only two possibilities that are not beyond the bounds of common sense.

The analysis of testing procedures thus far has disregarded the effects of rational minimization on the part of students. Let us repair this omission. We have seen that several techniques are available rationally to present essay answers that reduce the amount of information required. All of these methods, however, require some degree of ability to organize data with some coherence. Misdirection, for example, while it is at its best when it appears artless, does require a modicum of ability to unify ideas and present them in an orderly manner. The net effect of essay questions, then, is to provide a premium for the ability to integrate data.

Objective testing, on the other hand, tends to test each datum in isolation from other data. It is this method which rationalizes such memorization techniques as the use of review books and prepared summaries. For the objective test lends itself easily to mechanization; answers can be signaled or marked mechanically once a template has been constructed with no further necessity for consideration of the question that has provoked the choice. The ease of conveyance of information is a boon to specialization. Students will be much encouraged to organize activity where the results of such organization are patent.

Objective testing will, therefore, supplant essay testing on the grounds both that it decreases the rejection-to-acceptance ratio for a fixed amount of information and that it allows for more effective minimization of time and effort.

It should not be concluded from the above discussion that objective testing is the ultimate method of evaluation. While it enjoys the advantages cited, it does, in fact, not go far enough to be suitable for advanced stages of the development of educational institutions. The competition of institutions and the exigencies of political life have increased the student body to the point where objective testing has been unable to provide a sufficiently low ratio. It has until now found no rival. Such deficiencies as have become manifest have to be repaired by patchwork. A system of bonus points have been resorted to in some instances. In others, a series of questions, the answers to which are a matter of common knowledge, are used. In still other instances, scores are placed on a normal curve. This provides for a fixed number of rejections. Even this number, however, has proved too large for common use. It may be that a more realistic curve can be discovered for this purpose which will be less bound to the fetish of symmetry.

It may be thought that the sequential progression of modes of testing is arbitrary, or that the circumstances are unique to the educational field. A cursory glance at the history of quiz shows will serve to demonstrate the rigor with which the process proceeds in an area in which the necessary interests are present. By a happy chance, it was discovered that audiences are interested in quiz programs. The earliest of these were on the model of *Information, Please,* where cultural questions were asked of a panel of putative experts. These would discuss the implications of the question, occasionally at length. Early theoretical analyses assumed that members of the audience sympathized with the person submitting the question, presumably a person having more in common with the ordinary listener. More sophisticated investigation, however, showed that the audience identified with the person being asked the question.

As the popularity of the program led to much imitation, the

format of quiz programs began to change. The inclusion of persons of popular notoriety on the panels made the casual discussion of learned matter impossible. Questions became objective.

In time, even this proved inadequate. Quiz programs began to branch into several directions. In some cases, questions were made less difficult to the point where a fixed proportion of contestants, no longer purporting to be experts, could expect to answer correctly. In other cases, contestants were given advance information on the answers. In still other instances, the reward for failure was increased to the point where little disappointment was felt when the contestant could not answer the question. Each of these methods, while varying in approach, did meet the necessity for rewarding those who would not have been able to succeed in earlier formats. The sequence, from essay testing to objective testing, to giveaway testing, follows in main outline the progression of testing in the educational system.

Our analysis of institutional mechanics might continue into other areas, but it has by this point become obvious that these practices form a pattern. In each case the institution is rationally motivated to make those choices that maximize its profit and increase the size of its student body, by maintaining the prestige of its diploma relative to the cost. The course of action best suited for this is the cooperation with student minimizing techniques. The institutions are in the position of the auto companies when Henry Ford entered the field. Other companies, in order to maintain their own position, were forced to mass produce. Only when the market for the basic product was saturated could the manufacture of custom-made variations become profitable. In a saturated market, there is some scope for special products, for example, air-conditioned, bar-equipped cars, but it is relatively small. Institutions are forced to reduce the cost to the consumer in order to compete. Nevertheless, the reduction of cost must be sufficiently gradual that the prestige of the diploma is not upset. In education, cooperation with student mini-max procedures is the method.

The necessary progressive widening of the market follows definite economic laws. A new item on the market is high priced. It is adopted by the richest class. In time, all of this class have bought the item. The adjacent class demands it. The dropping sales to the richest class, by now saturated, combine with improvements in production methods to lower the price. The adjacent class purchases the item. By a series of scalloping curves, the item spreads until the entire market is saturated. Thus far, the picture has been drawn from Duesenberry.

Note, however, what happens to the prestige of the item in its orderly invasion of the marketplace. Early in the game, the item enjoys a marked differentiating prestige. As it spreads, it loses this prestige, differentiating between ever lower groups. When it reaches the saturation point, it differentiates only between normal consumers and marginal people. Television sets or cars, for example, have reached this point. The products, however, become prestige necessities rather than prestige luxuries.

The maintenance of prestige, to which so much attention is paid by manufacturers, is to a large degree beyond their control. The forces of the marketplace dictate the expansion of the market generally. Manufacturers' interest prevents a rapid drop in prestige through premature mass marketing; competition prevents the retention of a small upper-class market.

This is, in fact, the situation in education. Secondary education has a virtually saturated market. It is a prestige necessity. The college education market is in approximately the position of the automobile market shortly after Ford. It has begun reaching inexorably toward saturation. Graduate school education is still, by and large, not a mass-produced operation.

Of necessity, the prestige enjoyed by workers in an item declines with the expansion of the market. Auto dealers and high school teachers no longer enjoy the standing they once possessed by virtue of association with the rich and well-born. College professors are entering the same decline. As we will note later, this side effect of the operation of the market will have particular effect on the faculty.

8

The Faculty

It is of the essence of the educational bargain that the administration provide the student with a modicum of prestige. In general, the student does not have this prestige when he begins the educational transaction. He acquires it in two ways. Primarily, he undergoes a series of formalized contacts with a group of people who already have prestige. Secondarily, these prestiged persons must have an opportunity to observe his actions so that they can certify that he is worthy to receive the prestige token. This secondary method is, indeed, largely formal, since, as we have seen, the institution is required for rational reasons to award the token to all those who opt the educational quality, so long as they do not publicly bring the diploma into disrepute.

The institution, in order to fulfill its share of the educational bargain, must then maintain a staff of prestiged persons. It would be a strain on the finances of most institutions to maintain any sizable number of prestiged persons. However, the educational institution enjoys a considerable advantage in that it is precisely these institutions that set the criteria for prestige. The educational institution is then in the fortunate circumstance of being able to use its own products. It is part of a closed system.

The staff or prestiged persons is the faculty. As the services required of this staff determine its role in the educational process, we must examine in some detail the nature and extent of these services to show their effects on the various participants in the bargain.

Primary service required of a faculty member is his presence at regularly scheduled contacts with a number of students. In keeping with the serious nature of education these contacts should not be primarily social. It is a sizable advantage that there be some official task to which faculty members and students may address themselves. It keeps the contact from becoming too personal, which would serve as a source of embarrassment to both professor and students.*

In general, these periods of scheduled contact take the form of lectures. These constitute some nine to eighteen hours a week for professors, the time scheduled being referred to as the teaching load. The comparatively small number of hours when the attendance of the faculty member is required gives rise to problems in some cultures. In present-day American society it is considered a necessary condition for enjoying self-respect and the respect of others that one possess a full-time job. This may, perhaps, be the remnants of some Puritan strain in American culture. Until some two centuries ago, such moralistic strains were tempered by the aristocratic spirit, which approved of a life devoted to leisure or to martial exploits. With the rise of democracy, however, a life devoted to the full-time pursuit of gain enjoys the sole approved status.

Most full-time salaried jobs today require attendance some

* Paul Goodman is extremely sensitive to the advantages of the system of education in avoiding personal contact between professor and student. He attributes this to an avoidance of embarrassment on the professor's part, however. He is, unfortunately, less sensitive to the possible sources of embarrassment on the student's part, possibly because of an overidealized picture of the student. See Paul Goodman, *The Community of Scholars* (New York: Random House, Inc., 1962).

thirty-five to forty hours a week. Those who expect to maintain themselves in the executive class usually devote some eighty or ninety hours a week to the job. In these terms, the conventional evaluations of the present culture, the faculty member's job would be considered part-time.

Such a situation, however, would be unacceptable to the educational institution, for the employment of part-time faculty members would lend insufficient luster to the name of the institution. The institution is in the position of desiring the full time of the professor for services that require only part of his time. A number of peculiarities of the educational system can be understood as functional attempts to reconcile the needs of the institution for prestige with the small demands on the faculty member's time.

For example, it is a currently accepted legend that the professor devotes blocks of time to preparation for his lectures. This myth has some foundation in fact. The neophyte professor often fusses with his oration, both in redrafting it and in worrying about its effect on his hearers. Professors with a few years' experience soon arrive at a version satisfactory to themselves, and cease troubling themselves about its reception.

The professor, it must be remembered, enjoys the advantages of a vaudeville trouper compared to a TV performer. The former can continue to use the same material for years, confident that the bulk of his audience is new to him. The professor may enjoy equal confidence, since institutional rules prohibit repetitive purchase of the same subbargain. With the exception of some few students who fail to complete the subbargain in previous years and are so entitled to repeat their efforts, all students are new to the series.

It is commonly maintained that the professor, in addition to recasting his lecture notes periodically, rereads his lecture notes in order to polish his performance. Such theorizing, however, allows no scope to the virtuosity of the professor. Professors of some experience acquire the abilities of other performers which enables them to step immediately onto the stage and slip into their accustomed roles. The professor, indeed, has somewhat the advantage in that he is not only permitted but encouraged to refer constantly to notes. In fine, he enjoys the prompting machine of the TV performer with the low pressure of the vaudeville trouper.

Under these circumstances, the professor's primary requirement of scheduled contact with the students cannot be assumed to take up any large proportion of his working day. Let us then examine the situation in regard to the professor's secondary service, observation of the student's action to the point of certification of his worthiness to receive the token. As we have seen, this is largely formal. While the professor is in a position to certify worthiness, he is in no position to refrain from this certification. Nonetheless, we cannot assume merely on the basis of the pointlessness of an action from an official point of view that the action will not take place. Observation may indeed serve a latent function. Insofar as such observation occupies a sizable bulk of faculty time, it eases the discrepancy between the institution's need for prestige and the small demand on the faculty member's time.

In practice, observation consists largely of testing. We have already noted the tendency of testing to shift from essay questions to true-and-false and multiple-choice questions to giveaway questions. While these changes have been rational from the point of view of student and administration, we have not examined their effects on the faculty. The primary effect is in the time required to evaluate the results of a test. Notoriously the use of true-and-false or multiple-choice questions simplifies and accelerates the process of marking. Hoffman suggests that multiple-choice tests be called child-gradable tests to illustrate the ease of marking.[1] In any event, tests of this sort cannot be expected to occupy for long periods of time the attentions of faculty members.

The theory of giveaway testing has not been developed to the point where reliable empirical data is available on the time or effort required to mark these tests. However, insofar as students have some awareness of the degree of latitude extended by these tests, they are scarcely in a position to quarrel with the results. Faculty members should be under no constraint other than their own sense of duty to spend large amounts of time in grading these productions.

Whatever the nature of the tests used, however, the professor, if he chooses, may spend time perusing the student productions and criticizing or evaluating them. There are several considerations that tend to limit the amount of time spent in this pursuit, however.

Firstly, time spent in examining student productions is not highly visible. It cannot, then, add greatly to the prestige of either professor or institution. Of necessity, activities that are visible are at a premium compared to perusal of student presentations.

Secondly, perusal of student presentations is liable to interfere with student mini-max procedures. The net effect of such interference is an increase of difficulty per unit for the student. Since students are rationally motivated to reduce their difficulty per unit, a large increase tends, with time, to reduce the number of students opting the particular subbargain. Since the time spent in perusal is to some extent a function of the number of students opting the subbargain, there is a tendency for the number of hours spent in perusal to find an equilibrium at the minimum point.

However elegant the mathematical mechanism involved in the tendency may be, circumstances rarely allow it to reach its logical conclusion, which would result in leaving perusing professors totally devoid of students. For one thing, certain subbargains are mandatory in most institutions. These are exempt from the effects of the minimization law, except where more than one professor is allowed to negotiate the subbargain. For another thing, professors are loath to allow enrollment in the subbargain to fall to zero, although they may, on occasion, be satisfied to allow some decrease. More generally, they prefer increased enrollment. There is, then, some pressure exerted on the professor to limit interference with mini-max procedures; the net effect of this pressure is to reduce the time spent in perusal.

The analysis of the nature of perusal to mini-max procedures, however, has proceeded on the assumption that equal time spent in perusal produces equal difficulty for the student. This is true only as a rough generalization. Where a professor is able to peruse student productions without choosing to make such comments as would lead to an inference of his unwillingness to certify the subbargain, he is not increasing the difficulty. Perusal of this type is not, therefore, subject to automatic reduction. A professor, then, who finds that his periodic perusal is having adverse effects on the size of enrollment in his subbargains may switch to a less threatening variety of perusal.

The nonthreatening varieties of perusal enjoy another advantage, in addition to their comparative exemption from minimizing tendencies. Unquestionably the habit of critical examination is likely, to some degree, to slip over into the consideration of the productions of other faculty members. Where critical evaluation of other faculty members exists at present, it contributes to the marked tendency of the faculty to be divided into hostile cliques. Any increase in this tendency would add additional strain to an already tense atmosphere. Further, it would introduce a discrimination against the less intellectually gifted faculty members, which could sharply curtail the present democratic tendencies of the faculty. None of these results would be likely to enhance the reputation of the faculty of an institution in which they would appear.

It should be kept in mind that a prime rational motive for perusal is the appearance of educational activity. Professors are therefore able to utilize some mini-max procedures of their own to create the maximum appearance of perusal with the minimum of effort. It is a common practice, for example, to make careful notation of the first page of student production, scatter occasional comments through later pages, and add a few sentences at the end. Rarely is any note taken of the relevance of the comments.

More useful as a mini-max procedure is the careful assignment of dates for returning students' productions. Rational professors announce the return of student papers some two weeks after their presentation. While the actual perusal can be accomplished in an evening by a reasonably experienced professor, the length of the interval is taken as an indication of the amount of time devoted to perusal. This practice, however, has become so conventionalized as to lose much of its advantage. It is common to have a professor who has announced a two-week interval casually mention his perusal of the previous evening. Nevertheless, the student engaged in his own mini-max procedure will find it rational to ignore such occasional carelessness on the part of the professor.

As a result, then, of considerations of visibility and of interference with the smooth running of the institution, the time that the faculty devotes to activities relevant to lecturing is minimized. In part, this is possible because the professor enjoys a good deal of flexibility compared to persons outside the academic world. The number of hours per week that he is expected to devote to the institution by which he is employed is, except for his teaching load, not specified. Nor, with the same exception, is the location of his activities fixed. As a result of this, the variations in the amount and kind of services different professors provide are greater than are likely to be found in other employment. The professor, further, works largely without supervision, a condition rarely found outside of educational institutions. This latitude is highly prized in educational institutions, where it goes by the name of academic freedom. The ambiguity as to the nature of the faculty's work and the lack of a fixed location for this work make it difficult to say with any precision whether a faculty member is or is not earning his salary. Nonetheless, the faculty member himself will have some awareness of his status in this regard and will be, to a greater or lesser extent, disturbed by a failure to meet his own standards. While this pressure is considerably less than the suasion exerted on an office worker who sits idle in a business establishment during working hours, we may look to the latter to examine his technique for dealing with the problem in the expectation that correlates will be found in the academic world.

First, business to hand may be dealt with summarily or can be handled at length, almost lovingly. The latter technique has obvious advantages under conditions of what we may term underemployment. The use of such extension of legitimate activities to the point where it is conspicuous is technically called goldbricking. Much of the apparently uneconomical use of perusal time may be understood as rational in this context. The professor is thus motivated to resist the mechanism tending toward minimization of perusal time and to adopt the nonthreatening type of perusal to avoid the effects of minimization.

Except in the hands of an expert, the time consumed by leisurely handling of the business at hand is limited. It is convenient, then, in offices, to devote remaining company time to some business of the company which, while strictly speaking not the affair of the worker, can be discussed at length with the appearance of forwarding the company's interest. Thus, underemployed workers often take to writing lengthy memoranda or indulging in protracted lectures on how other workers should conduct their jobs. For the sake of avoidance of rancorous controversy, it is usually advisable to direct these literary efforts to the activities of workers who are not underemployed and thus do not have the leisure for spirited replies.

Such quasi-supervisory activities also have their limits when pursued individually. The use of a committee, however, extends the limits considerably.[2] Where an individual may take an afternoon to write a report, a committee of twenty taking an afternoon absorbs some hundred man hours. Still more advantageously, they are less likely at the end of this time to have completed their report. More often, they have discovered several factions who disagree about the contents of the report and require several additional sessions to hammer out an agreeable compromise.

Faculty members have not been laggard in their discovery of the advantages of committee work. Committees devoted to all aspects of academic work abound. For the faculty, committee work has the additional advantage of high visibility. Time spent in this way both contributes to the prestige of the members and lends an air of active enterprise to the university. Caplow and McGee in *The Academic Marketplace*[3] discuss the use of committee procedures in hiring staff: "When we examined the specific procedures of hiring in the American university, they turned out to be almost unbelievably elaborate. The average salary of an assistant professor is approximately that of an average bakery truck driver and his occupancy of the job to be less permanent. Yet it may require a large part of the time of twenty highly skilled men for a full year to hire him." The authors also discover that such apparently cumbrous proceedings are current for the hiring of teaching assistants, whose stay is even more transient and whose effect on the prestige of the institution is negligible. Caplow and McGee are somewhat at a loss to explain these methods of handling business, apparently since they contrast the method with a picture of outside business practices which is highly idealized.

All the activities listed above can be characterized, at least theoretically, as primarily entered into for the sake of the institution. Since the duties of a faculty member are loosely defined, he is free to enter into a number of activities that benefit the institution secondarily and to pass them off as part of his official activities, the more so as some of them are more valuable to the institution than activities primarily devoted to its benefit.

Of these activities, the writing of books or scholarly articles for publication is the most prestigious. The primary beneficiary of such publications is the author. While the publication of any single article or book is unlikely to make much difference, the accumulation of a sufficient number, as in the Indian custom of counting coups, entitles a man to some respect. In general, a professor with a number of publications to his credit has greater mobility. The increased possibility of finding a more satisfactory position in another institution is a useful bargaining point in negotiating with the professor's own administration, although it is rarely as efficacious as faculty legend would have it. Similarly, while an institution derives little benefit from the presence of one or two writers, although they may be used as token exhibits, the reputation of having a large number of faculty members with publications to their credit adds definite prestige.

The exact status of this prestigious activity remains ideologically unclear. It is often dependent on the attitude taken toward the official function of an educational institution. For millennia the relative position of the research and learning function as compared to the teaching function has been hotly debated on campus; nor is there any indication that the next millennium will see less discussion or more clarification. Generally, professorial writers, such as Veblen,[4] see the production of learned works as the chief function of the university, howbeit few take so extreme a position, while those who have more difficulty in publishing maintain the teaching function side of the argument. By common consent of the faculty, the claims of the writers to be serving a legitimate educational function is accepted. The attitude of the administration varies in accordance with some complex laws, which we will examine more closely in a later chapter.

If the attitude of the administration toward publication seems ambivalent, it is more generous toward outside employment. Where the outside employment can be viewed as part-time, for example, as a consultantship, the administrative blessing is generally forthcoming. Activity of this sort has less visibility than publication, but the local notoriety of being consultant to some large corporation is appreciated. The growth of this pattern of quasi-official moonlighting has had important consequences in educational institutions.

First, consultantships are lucrative. The professor who manages to obtain one or more—and, as usual, these desiderata are more likely to go to those who have than to those who do not—often finds that he is earning more on his secondary job than in his primary occupation. Under these circumstances most people would switch occupations, specializing in the more lucrative. Although this does happen, of course, it is not so easily accomplished. Often the business consultantship is based paradoxically on the fact that the professor is not in the business world. It is then necessary to retain the primary job to maintain the secondary. Under these circumstances, the professor's academic job may be seen as a holding position, while the focus of attention is on the consultantship. This offers a signal advantage to the administration, who enjoy extra leeway in dealing with the faculty member. He does not have the same interest in his institutional salary as a man who is dependent on his professorial pay to support his family. The institution, in such cases, enjoys the position of business concerns in the suburbs, who hire housewives in the knowledge that the pay is seen as a secondary source of income to the worker, with the result that pay scales are appreciably lower.

Where even a few members of the faculty hold consultantships, the ramifications spread through the faculty. For the happy few are rationally motivated to adopt a different attitude toward faculty negotiations with the administration. Those members who are primarily dependent on faculty salary are under great pressure to procure increases, while those holding consultantships are motivated to avoid menacing a position whose chief advantage is its existence for the sake of a very limited gain. With such disparate attitudes, faculty unity is difficult to maintain. Professors without consultantships then enjoy a salary to some degree lower than they might have had were no consultantships permitted. They are then likely to adopt the high position that the prestige of the university and of academic life in general should not permit professors to indulge in such mercenary avocations. Retorts to this attitude are not hard come by. Faculty harmony is not augmented in the process.

While consultantships, being held off the institutional premises, are only of secondary benefit to the university, professors will, on occasion, have access to another source of income, more valuable to the institution. Corporations, foundations, and governmental departments offer increasingly large numbers of research grants. These are customarily awarded to faculty members. The extent of the grants vary, the larger grants running into considerable amounts of money. For these, equipment of various kinds and complexities are required. The institution is able to profit in various ways. To begin with, a fixed percentage of the grant, often 15 per cent, is paid to the institution for overhead. This amount is virtually pure profit, as the space would otherwise, in all probability, lie fallow. In addition, special charges are made for secretarial aid and for materials of all sorts. Astute bursars rarely lose money on such negotiations. Where specialized equipment is necessary, it is usually paid for by the grant and reverts to the institution when the grant terminates. If the grant is large enough, it provides supplementary employment for several professors. Since the institution has some say in their choice, it is in the doubly advantageous position of employer and institutional beneficiary. Understandably, the institution has a large stake in research grants.

The professor who is in a position to bring such educational advantages to an institution can negotiate with the administration on terms far different from those of most of his colleagues. While he enjoys along with his consultant brethren the advantages of a double salary—and he may also be a consultant himself —he is able to use his secondary job to increase the advantages of his primary position. He will find it greatly to his advantage to negotiate separately with the institution.

As a result, then, of varying secondary positions held by the faculty, the range of faculty salaries is extensive. While those who are the most dependent on this salary are highly motivated to seek uniform payment, those with the greater bargaining power are rationally inclined to allow the laws of supply and demand a freer hand. In point of fact, market values do have the larger role in setting work conditions for the faculty. It is common among faculty have-nots to accuse the administration of playing off one faculty member against another. In most instances, such a policy on the part of the administration would be quite unnecessary.

While we have gone into some detail in discussing the position of those faculty members with some advantages accruing from circumstances outside the institution, it must be remembered that these represent comparatively few faculty members, although their effect is out of proportion to their numbers. By far the majority of faculty members lack the outside contacts that would enable them to pursue a dual role.

For most of the faculty, then, work consists of academic duties. As we have seen, these duties need be neither onerous nor time consuming. As a result, faculty members have both the leisure to debate questions of interest and the difficulty of justifying a comparative lack of activity to a culture that considers a modicum of activity a necessary condition for moral virtue. In general, a concern with trivia and a degree of acrimony in the discussion of the relevant questions, in fine, pettiness, is characteristic of those whose time is not fully occupied. Housewives, for example, are notorious for precisely those characteristics that form the most frequent accusations against faculty members. The same tendencies in housewives, however, are viewed with a degree of charity rarely accorded to professors. Paradoxically, the very harshness of the criticism of professors tends to increase the attributes criticized.

What is operating here is a circular process. The faculty's unhappiness over working few hours in a society where a long working day is equated with virtue leads to behavior that further incurs the disapproval of society. The greater the disapproval, the more extreme the behavior. It is difficult to see under what circumstances this circular action could be disrupted. So long as the nature of professorial duties remains substantially as it is at present, in marked contrast with expected behavior in other industries, conflict is to be expected. There is little reason to anticipate any change in the duties of faculty, as these derive necessarily from the structure of education. We may, however, consider the possibilities of changes in the outside world.

There is a group of sociologists and economists whose analyses are predicated on the notion of the affluent society. Basically, this group concludes that it is now within the realm of possibility for the present technology to satisfy all of man's necessities and a reasonable number of luxuries. The curve of technological improvement is extrapolated into the future to the point where a substantial degree of luxury is visualized as within the grasp of the common man. In this situation, it is conceivable that workers will prefer a shorter work week to a higher degree of luxury. It is hardly to be expected that in the foreseeable future the ordinary workingman will be able to afford as short a work week as is common in education. Nevertheless, to the extent that the ordinary work week is shortened, the disapproval of faculty members will be mitigated. It is reasonable to expect that the behavior of faculty members under such circumstances will be less extreme.

9

Renegotiation

Thus far we have analyzed the negotiation of the educational bargain where, despite the comparative absence of escalation into the power dimension, the power differential has had its effect in determining the point at which the bargain is struck and have investigated the sources of elasticity in the contract. As we have seen, although the educational contract tends to be elastic, this elasticity is not infinite. In the ultimate analysis, a participant to a contract can determine its elasticity only by trial and error. Since each participant stands to gain by making maximum use of the elasticity, obviously participants must find themselves, at times, on the far side of the vague border that marks the limit of elasticity. At such a point either a breach of contract or renegotiation ensues.

Such renegotiations are somewhat more tension-provoking than the original bargain. The parties to the original bargain, negotiating for a proposed advantage on both sides, have not, in fact, made any investment in the bargain before the bargain is struck. They have, therefore, nothing to lose except some hopes of possible advantage to be gained from the bargain. During renegotiation, both sides have, to varying degrees, committed their resources to the successful fulfillment of the contract by the other party. A contract terminated without such fulfillment represents, to varying degrees, a loss. As the stakes in such renegotiation are correspondingly higher, the willingness of each party to escalate to higher levels is correspondingly stronger.

Likewise, renegotiation occurs under sporadic and unplanned conditions, when one of the parties happens to overestimate the elasticity of the contract. Renegotiation is, therefore, an individual matter, not subject to the same type of standardization prevailing in negotiation. The particular form that renegotiation takes may be heavily influenced by the nature of the clauses of the contract whose violation is in question. Nevertheless, we should be able to observe certain regularities in the proceedings. We may begin by evaluating the power positions of the participants at the time of renegotiation.

On the purely economic level, the educational institution enjoys certain contractual advantages. The original bargain has provided that the major consideration involved, the granting of the prestige token, occurs only subsequent to the student's fulfillment of his contractual obligations. The student has, therefore, a considerably heavier commitment to the successful fulfillment of the contract than the institution. This would be true in any case because of the polypolistic nature of the educational market, where one institution deals with a large number of individual participants. The particular nature of the individual contract, however, makes this advantage considerably more extreme.

In any form of contract negotiation, the extent of damage to be suffered by the termination of a contract without fulfillment of contractual obligations is a function of the willingness of alternative partners to negotiate contracts under favorable terms. In a highly competitive market, the eagerness of alternative partners to negotiate tends to minimize the damage to be suffered from the breakdown of negotiations in regard to any individual contract. As we have seen, the competitiveness of the market is contingent upon the adoption by the government of a strategy of intervention conducive to high competitiveness.

In the marketplace for most tangible goods in the United States, the government is committed to a strategy of not permitting control of the market to rest within a few hands. This commitment has extended to the point of promising intervention against any widespread agreements for the fixing of prices. These are automatically deemed collusive agreements in restraint of trade. Although this strategy is no guarantee that such agreements will not take place, their negotiation is conducted gingerly and with due regard for the decorum of secrecy. In practice, the execution of such agreements is fraught with peril and the temptation for violation of agreement correspondingly high. If the threat of government intervention does not succeed in fomenting a marketplace of competition, it enjoys, at least, the relative success of imposing considerable barriers to the easy organization of the market.

In the educational enclave, the government has not opted to pursue a similar strategy. Educational institutions freely hold conventions which differ from the associations of the major vendors of tangible goods only in regard to the absence of secrecy in the proceedings. While these conventions arrange for gentlemen's agreements on the nature of contracts to be negotiated by educational institutions, they are held under conditions of no more secrecy than that afforded by the technical nature of the discussion. There is not only no preoccupation with the possibility of governmental intervention designed to hinder the organization of the enclave, but, on the contrary, every expectation that any governmental intervention will, in fact, be with the intention of aiding further the process of organization.

Given, then, the degree of organization of the educational enclave feasible under this strategy, a student faced with the termination of contract without the award of the prestige token is in a somewhat difficult position. The most prestigious institutions, which would ordinarily be the most acceptable alternative partners for new contracts, tend to be committed by their close relationships with the theoretically independent educational institution that has terminated the contract. Since the enclave is still imperfectly organized, the student can usually find some smaller institution willing, in a specific case, to risk the displeasure of the giants in the field. While such a proceeding on the part of the student enables him to cut his losses, the necessity to conclude further bargains with what are essentially marginal firms automatically assures him of some prestige loss even under the most favorable circumstances.

Even the willingness of an alternative institution to enter into a bargain, however, does not mean that the student's loss is limited to that accounted for by the prestige differential between the institutions involved. The student is not seeking a contract equivalent to those negotiated with potential partners with no previous investment in education on the level in question. He hopes for a bargain that recognizes his previous investment as legitimate fulfillment of his contractual obligations to date. In practice, most institutions negotiating bargains with terminating students tend to discount heavily his previous fulfillments.

This process of discounting offers several advantages to the educational institution which serves as a prospective partner. First, it enables the institution to maintain a far more flexible policy than that which would be afforded by the simple acceptance or rejection of a contract. The negotiation of a heavily discounted contract allows the institution to garner the advantages to be accrued from the prestige contributions of the student partner while still answering charges from other institutions of having failed to contribute its share to the organization in the market. Second, a policy of heavy discounting invites reciprocity on the part of other institutions. The knowledge among the students that the extent of their fulfillment of the contract would be accepted by other institutions only with heavy discounting is sufficient to discourage precipitate termination of contract.

In fact, reciprocity of discounting is not only not the case, but, for the majority of educational institutions, not particularly desirable. For the majority of institutions use the extent of discounting as an index of prestige. The ability of a particular institution to discount more heavily the extent of fulfillment than its competitors is taken as prima facie evidence that the institution is more prestigious. This serves as an escape valve for competitive tendencies within a rather organized market. The situation is rather analogous to that analyzed by Machlup for polypolies in the tangible market where competition in packaging and advertising serves to channelize aggressive impulses and permit noncompetitive stability of product design and pricing.[1]

In any event, the institution enjoys the economic advantage that termination of contract is likely to prove economically damaging to the student's prior investment in the educational bargain. As may be expected, from any particular advantage, its influence extends far beyond its use. In most renegotiations the threat of its use is sufficient to terminate renegotiation at a point favorable to the institution. In fact, the institution enjoys the use of a graded series of responses of which termination is the most extreme. The institution may refuse to recognize the fulfillment by the student of some of its subbargains, or, more flexibly, threaten to withhold such recognition.

The effectiveness of this process as a deterrent to effective negotiation lies more in the lack of information about the realistic prospects. Students do not normally expect to seek new contracts. Where a faculty member may well consider a move as simply a speeding up of a scheduled action, the student is more likely to see transfer of contract as an interference with the programed plan of education. The typical student has few contacts with other institutions and is likely to be emotionally involved with his alma mater. Educational institutions in the United States have often seen fit to act *in loco parentis,* and attempts at paternalism are often taken at face value. Administrative officials find it convenient to treat difficulties between student and administration as though they were personal problems of the student, making free with advice, which would in other circumstances be questioned as coming from an interested party. Such attitudes on the part of the institution are not limited to students, but must be assayed with faculty members on an individual basis, there being a highly vocal, if small minority of faculty members who will insist on being treated as adults.

The institution, in addition, enjoys the economic advantage of a superior moral position. The bulk of the institution's contractual obligations, those involved in the granting of the prestige token, fall due subsequent to any particular renegotiation. The only obligations of the institution that can come into question at the time of renegotiation is its obligation to provide the student with a number of prestigious persons from whom he can acquire prestige through leakage. As we have seen, however, the institution enjoys the advantage of being able on its own to certify the prestigious quality of the persons it supplies. The possibility, then, that the institution can be legitimately accused of nonfulfillment of contract is negligible.

The student, on the other hand, is committed to a series of obligations to do various acts designed to maintain and augment the prestige position of the educational institution. As we have seen in previous chapters, these obligations are open to varying interpretations. The educational institution is, at various points, rationally motivated to treat these clauses with extreme elasticity. In most cases, the bulk of nonfulfillment has been acceded to by the institution only tacitly. It enjoys the luxury of maintaining its ignorance of states of affairs which exist in violation of the written clauses of the contract. The student, in fact, finds it impossible to document evidence of the previous collusion of the institution with elastic practices. During the process of renegotiation, the student finds himself on the defensive and thereby likely to conclude renegotiation at a point less favorable than bargaining conditions would warrant.

In the ordinary course of events, these economic advantages are sufficient to enable the institution to conclude renegotiation on favorable terms. Where this is not the case, the higher stakes in renegotiation facilitate escalation into the power dimension. Let us, then, consider the power advantages available to the institution.

Institutions normally maintain a small staff of mercenaries. These are usually provided with small arms to the degree generally compatible with the extent of armaments considered legitimate for the protection of private property. In emergency situations, the institution has access to a larger staff of personnel whose primary task is the physical maintenance of the educational plant. This force is generally sufficient for dealing with disturbances on the part of a few individuals, but totally inadequate to handle large-scale problems. It is neither trained nor equipped for riot control. While educational institutions undoubtedly possess the economic resources that would permit of far more extensive development of the possibilities inherent in the maintenance of their own armed forces, few institutions have taken advantage of these possibilities.

In large part, the institution's previous high degree of success with economic advantage has inhibited the appropriate development of a staff adequate to the appropriate use of force in contract negotiation. Furthermore, economic considerations have limited the willingness of institutional administrations to invest in a form of bargaining power so rarely used. As a result, the institution's use of force has practically fallen into desuetude. While the general lack of preparedness on the part of the university has aided its budgetary flexibility, the tactical consequences have been somewhat deleterious. Our earlier study of power theory showed that the most efficient use of force is rather the threat of force than the actual practice of it. Nevertheless, the threat is effective only insofar as it possesses credibility. The general underdevelopment of institutional defense forces has severely vitiated the credibility of any institutional threat to make use of them. As a result, institutions in renegotiation are compelled to escalate directly from economic action to the threat to manipulate governmental intervention successfully. This has, in fact, been the practice.

The threat to solicit government intervention is, as we have seen, contingent on the probability of such intervention and the likelihood that such intervention, if undertaken, will bring results favorable to the soliciting party. Let us consider the latter contingency first.

In general, institutions presume that intervention on the part of the government will be in their favor. Government spokesmen generally issue statements indicating extensive sympathy with education. These are usually taken to indicate the favorable attitude toward the institutions that embody this societal value. It is, again, generally assumed that the government's approval of education does not extend to the students or the faculty. As with all government commitments, certainty is possible only after the fact. The degree of obscurity that characterizes governmental strategic commitments is even more conspicuous than usual in those relating to the educational enclave. Nevertheless, the government's continuing interest in educational affairs is evidenced by its maintenance of large-scale enterprises in this field, a practice in which it indulges in very few markets. Within these enterprises the government has invariably taken the institutional role. Many of the personnel who have worked for the government as part of the administrative bureaucracy of one or another of the government educational institutions have subsequently transferred to other parts of the government bureaucracy and might reasonably be assumed to have taken with them the habits of mind cultivated in their previous employment. Of course, the government employs, as well, a number of ex-students. The habits of mind acquired as a student seem little likely to encourage active intervention, however.

Furthermore, government strategy toward the organization of the academic enclave, previously cited in the discussion of the institution's economic advantages, has rather uniformly favored educational institutions. The logical extrapolation of this preference to more active questions of renegotiation would lead the impartial observer to predict a similar sympathy.

Any hesitation on the part of the educational institution to invoke governmental intervention has not been the result of a lack of confidence in the generally favorable effects of such intervention. While the matter admits of no certainty, a reasonably sanguine institutional administrator is extremely likely to consider it a good bet.

The inhibition to the more frequent use of the threat of governmental intervention resides, rather, in the uncertainty in regard to the possibility of the intervention actually occurring. Government policy tends, like all rational policies in this area, to be oriented to the minimal use of power. As a result, the government prefers to use the threat of force to actual force in its intervention. The response, then, to institutional solicitation is likely to be rather an attempt to negotiate with the parties involved than a direct resort to force. Even where the outcome of such intervention is favorable, the absence of a demonstration of force is likely to prejudice the credibility of the institution's threat to manage intervention successfully.

The principal checks to the actual use of power are traditionally the absence of detection, the failure of power, or the failure of nerve. In the case under consideration, the solicitation of intervention precludes any great hope that detection can be avoided. The state of the government's armed forces, while occasionally of dubious adequacy for dealing with the armed forces of a rival State, are ordinarily more than sufficient for the management of the citizens. There can be little doubt that a government willing to commit as large a portion of its armed forces as is necessary for a specific intervention directed toward the improvement of one of its enclaves can achieve its goal. It is rather the third contingency that is most problematic. Governments are conventionally overthrown for their unwillingness to commit sufficient force at crucial moments. Although a government that resorts to negotiation in situations in which it has committed itself to immediate armed intervention risks its own credibility, it is a matter of history that governments have been prone to this miscalculation. Educational institutions, then, considering the use of an appeal to government intervention, must weigh the possibility that the proposed solicitation will turn out to reveal the government's weakness rather than its strength.

What is in question in cases of government intervention is usually not the suppression of a riot situation, but the subsequent punishment of one of the parties. It is in regard to this latter that governments tend to be negligent. Yet the absence of subsequent punishment turns out not only to fail to deter future riots, but to actually encourage repetition of the strategy. The current government trend to replace long-term intervention by the writing of reports by social scientists explaining the causes of disturbances in terms of the dissatisfactions of the rioters tends to nullify what few steps the government has taken toward the achievement of its goals during the short-term repression of the riots.

Summing up, the administration enjoys sizable economic advantages, some limited possibilities in the direct use of force, an ease in invoking government intervention that will be favorably motivated but may be highly ineffective.

The student's bargaining position, in economic terms, is limited. As a single student, he will be at a major disadvantage unless he enjoys the luxury of some powerful friends. The key to a more advantageous position is clearly organization. Given a situation that calls so clearly for collective bargaining, we must consider why student attempts at collective bargaining have been so limited.

To begin with, the students are not entirely without organization. In most institutions, it is customary for the students to elect a council, without ordinarily any specification of the interests that such a group is intended to represent. In point of fact, such bodies are usually social and honorific. Election to them is more on the basis of popularity than on leadership. Where collective bargaining does take place, leadership very often is *ad hoc*.

We have seen earlier that the tendency toward elasticity of contract has tended to encourage certain student associations. While these are undoubtedly more directly committed to student interests than the more formal bodies that purport to represent the students, their view of students' interests is such as to predispose them more to private collusion than to the more vigorous struggles of collective bargaining. Other social groupings among the students suffer from the same limitation.

Furthermore, the terms of the educational bargain are not such as to encourage collective bargaining. Bargains at the college level tend to be of fixed duration. For the most part, contracts are assumed to run four years. Students are thus rarely motivated to organize to better a contract that is reasonably short-range and unlikely to be renewed. The institution has the advantage; it is always negotiating contracts with only a portion of the student body and with that portion before it has a chance to get together and organize.

The contractual organization, moreover, of the student body into four cohorts tends to divide it into four status levels. While the distinction between these groups does not appear from the outside as a major significance, much is made of the difference by the students themselves. In the ordinary course of events, it is difficult for a newcomer to rise immediately to a position of leadership. Where he is automatically consigned to the lowest status category, difficulties are even greater. Leadership in student groups regularly devolves upon those close to the successful termination of their contracts. These are people who have the most to risk, either in renegotiation or in the termination of their contracts without the award of the prestige token. In the history of collective bargaining, it has traditionally been the leaders in bargaining whose contracts have been terminated after the bargain has been struck. Educational institutions have not been less prone to such a policy than business organizations in other enclaves. The leadership of student groups has a degree of caution built in by the particular nature of the educational contract.

The structure of the contract has also inhibited student organization in another respect. It has rendered leadership exceedingly transitory. Since the leaders selected are ordinarily within a year of termination of contract, it is exceedingly rare that student leadership extends beyond the calendar year. Activity in the educational enclave does not usually extend beyond some 50 per cent of the year. When we deduct the interruption involved in the jockeying of position for the leadership of the subsequent year, comparatively little time remains to be devoted to collective bargaining activity.

The history of collective bargaining in other enclaves shows that the bargaining situation has regularly elicited the rise of a professional leadership. While undoubtedly some of this leadership has been indigenous, other parts show only a token connection with the activities of the group being led. Yet, students have been notably retarded in their movement toward professionalization in this field. In part, this failure can be attributed to the relative absence of professional students. Until fairly recently, the number of people willing to make a career of being a student, rather than merely terminate their contract in four years, has been extremely limited. Perhaps the economy of scarcity, as in the past, tended to restrict this form of specialization to some extent.

The professionalization of leadership has also suffered from the peculiar economic nature of the educational contract. Most other enclaves develop contracts whose essential element is the payment of money. There have, thus, been sufficient reserves of currency to hire professional experts. The educational contract, on the other hand, revolves largely about the exchange of prestige. While prestige is exchangeable and transferable, it has nowhere reached the level of convertibility to compare with currency. Potential professional leadership has been highly loath to accept payment purely in terms of prestige. With, however, a rapidly rising standard of living, the economic resources of students are rapidly increasing. Today, it is probably even possible for students to collect sufficient funds to purchase professional organizational skills. It is probably a question of time before such becomes the practice.

It may be noted that, in regard to government strategy of intervention, the collective bargaining situation in the educational enclave resembles more the collective bargaining situation of a hundred years ago in other enclaves than it does their present situation. In the nineteenth century leaders of collective bargaining regularly counted on their contracts being terminated simultaneously with the termination of bargaining. In any event, they scarcely expected government intervention in their especial favor. In our own day, government intervention to protect the contract of leaders of collective bargaining is sufficiently common outside of the educational enclave, that its use is scarcely necessary. Thus far, the government has shown no inclination to bring its educational strategy into line with its commitments in other enclaves.

Under the circumstances, then, collective bargaining is fraught with difficulties for the students. Yet, the threat of a student strike is virtually the only economic advantage that the student possesses. The termination of contract by any single student is sufficiently unimportant to the educational institution as to be meaningless. Until recently it was held in student circles that the student might derive economic advantage from the threat of the use of publicity. Since administrative officers of educational institutions had taken great pains both to court favorable publicity and to suppress unfavorable, it was assumed that the object of so much careful concern needs must be of some importance. This impression was, perhaps, even more widely shared in administration circles. The efficacy of the threat in bargaining could be inferred from the rather rapid escalation in the power dimension with which it was countered.

Within recent years, a number of the major educational institutions have been subject to just such a spate of bad publicity as administrative officials had taken such extreme care to avoid. The results proved quite surprising. There were none. The absence of ill effects seems to have thoroughly refuted both the fears of the institutions and the hopes of the students. It has become apparent that the maintenance of a favorable image is of no more importance in the educational enclave than in other marketplaces.

In the comparative absence of strong economic arguments, considerations of power disparities become important in student bargaining. The limitations we have noted in the institutional use of direct force do not apply to student strikes. While the students have but rarely exercised their ability to use arms, their large number more than compensates for deficiencies in this respect. Of course, the students' use of force, like their use of economic advantage, is contingent upon a degree of organization. It is, however, rather less difficult to generate the organization necessary for the short-term use of force than for the more protracted arrangements of economic advantage. Organization for the use of force is likewise exempt from another of the limitations of the usual collective bargaining situation. While one must be a party to a contract to refrain from fulfilling it, any interested spectator can become a participant in the use of force. This permits student leadership to draw upon a wider constituency for the use of force than would be available for more prosaic collective bargaining.

As in other power appeals, the maximum effectiveness in the use of student force is attained by successful manipulation of its threat. In threatening force, the students enjoy a further advantage: there is little tendency to question their credibility. Administration officials who have devoted much energy over the years to castigating the irresponsibility of students almost invariably come, in time, to take their own words seriously. The institution's stereotype of the student is such as to consider him capable of any enormity. Administrators are, therefore, little inclined to doubt that even threats lightly made have a high probability of being implemented. Since the students maintain the advantage on the level of direct power by virtue of their extreme numerical superiority, such deterrents to the student use of force as exist are likely to be located at the level of government intervention.

Government strategy, in the area of the educational enclave, has not been such as to predispose student groups to invoke its aid. Student consideration of government intervention has been more devoted to the strategy for minimizing its effects than to the possibility of appealing for its support. Student tactics have tended toward the hope of concluding renegotiations immediately following the use of force. Where government intervention can be successfully delayed, its effect will be minimal. The government's general commitment to the minimum use of power has tended to inadvertently buttress this tactic.

The student position is, then, the reverse of that of the administration. The students are weak at the level of economic advantage, strong in their access to direct power, and weak in respect to government intervention, deriving their only advantage on this level from the hopes of government inefficiency.

Having catalogued the various assets and debits of the parties to the educational contract, we may now attempt to describe the course of renegotiation. Renegotiation ordinarily takes place when the institution decides to challenge the nonfulfillment of some clause of the contract. The administration considers the action as an individual negotiation between the institution and the particular student involved. Given the institution's economic advantage, it is likely to couch its economic appeal in the terms of an ultimatum. Since standard student tactics are oriented toward the evasion of onerous clauses rather than the more direct confrontation of renegotiation, these ultimatums are generally successful. Periodically, however, administration officials overestimate the elasticity of the educational contract. These circumstances normally provoke a more extensive process of renegotiation. The student in question attempts to seek the support of his fellows in the traditional forms of collective bargaining. Where such support is lacking, which may be fairly frequent in the light of the difficulties of collective bargaining cited above, the student either accedes to the ultimatum or attempts to negotiate a contract with some alternative educational institution.

Should the student meet with a modicum of success sufficient to indicate some reasonable probability of joint action on the part of at least an active minority of the student body, the counter-offer is likely to escalate immediately to the threat of force. This may be considered as terminating the first round of the negotiation.

Since strategy on the part of the educational institution assumes that student use of force suffers from no great limitation in respect to failure of nerve, the student counter-offer calls for an immediate response. The counter-offer having brought the renegotiation to the level of power, effective response requires an answer at this level at least. The institution is embarrassed by a comparative weakness at this level of renegotiation. Adequacy of response, therefore, requires further escalation. The institution's offer for the second round of negotiations is, therefore, conventionally a threat of appeal to governmental intervention. The students' response to this offer is contingent upon its credibility. While the students have no reason to doubt that the threatened solicitation will really occur, government response is invariably subject to a certain degree of uncertainty. The recent history of government intervention in renegotiation has done little to relieve this uncertainty. Given the general human tendency toward optimism in uncertain situations, the most probable counter-offer to be expected from the students, in the second round, is the forceful occupation of the institutional plant. For the first time in the process of renegotiation, the educational institution has committed an investment in the bargaining proceedings comparable in extent to the students' investment.

At this point, the institution is rationally committed to soliciting intervention and the government rationally committed to intervening. Whether such solicitation or intervention actually takes place remains problematic. Either institution or government may suffer a failure of nerve.

It would be hazardous, at this point in history, to predict the outcome of renegotiation processes that have escalated to such a degree. The number of such cases are small. Most renegotiations terminate during the first round with the inability of the student to achieve sufficient cooperation to make collective bargaining possible.

Generalization from negotiation proceedings in other enclaves suggest that long-range secular trends tend to characterize changes in the organization of an enclave. As one of the parties in an enclave begins to resort with some regularity to the previously unaccustomed use of force, the results of the first few major negotiations become crucial. Where the party is able to establish its regular willingness to follow the threat of force by the use of force, it succeeds in establishing the credibility of its threat. To the degree that such developments take place, the groundwork is laid for subsequent pacification. The successful establishment of the credibility of threats shifts the distribution of power toward the successful party. The unsuccessful party learns to expand its range of acceptable bargain to the point where overlap may occur without escalation. In schematic terms, this has been the history of collective bargaining in the economic enclave. Labor unions have succeeded in establishing the credibility of their threats. Management and government have succeeded in discrediting their threats. Inevitably, rational management has been driven to the extension of its range of acceptable bargain.

In the educational enclave the key issue is whether institutions and government will maintain the credibility of their threats, which have been put into question. A strategy of rapid and widespread action in accordance with strategic commitment will preserve the traditional point at which educational bargains are struck. Tardy and ineffective use of force will result in a shift in the laws governing the educational enclave similar to the secular shift that has taken place in the economic marketplace. In either event, we may expect that a period in which escalation is common will, as the results of escalation begin to form a pattern, be succeeded by a period of relative peace in which the effects of escalation will be felt without the necessity for its frequent recourse.

A number of recent events, in particular several that have made the front pages of the newspapers, have departed markedly from the paradigm of coercive bargaining sketched out here. Where, for example, what would appear to be the students' initial offer is a demand that institutional officials change the nation's foreign policy, it is difficult to understand such a request in any bargaining terms. Similarly, where institutional officials meet the terms of the student offer only to find that they are greeted with a counter-offer that rapidly reduces the area of acceptable bargain to a point that gives every evidence of being beyond the ability of the administration to expand, the situation would appear to be, on its face, a power struggle rather than a form of negotiation, coercive or otherwise. The theory upon which this book is based assumes that confrontation, while it may be a means toward moving the point at which a bargain is struck in the direction of one of the partners, does not become an end in itself. Where it has—and the actions as well as the rhetoric of some of the participants in the educational enclave indicate that it has—the resulting confrontation can no longer be considered as rational means for any of the ends considered as legitimate to the educational enclave.

Although these occurrences are certainly of interest to the sociologist as data for the study of the strategy of revolution, they are not relevant to the analysis of educational institutions any more than a description of sit-ins in Southern lunch counters are germane to a study of the restaurant business. That the particular occurrences took place within the educational plant can be attributed simply to the discovery on the part of the student that it was not necessary to undergo the onerous chore of traveling to a Mississippi hamburger stand or a Chicago Convention to express his opinion of the world in which his elders find themselves. Given the obvious convenience of organizing disturbances without traveling, it is to be expected that educational plants will continue to be one of the favorite loci of confrontations. Nonetheless, the participants to these edifying spectacles are not functioning as members of the educational enclave, but in their Jeffersonian capacity as citizens. Explanations of their conduct are beyond the scope of this book.

Thus far we have devoted our discussion of renegotiation to bargaining concerning the major educational contract: that between the institution and the students. It will be worth our while to devote some consideration to the details of renegotiation between institutions and faculty and, somewhat later in the chapter, the relationship between faculty and students.

Empirically, the administration enjoys a comparatively free hand vis-à-vis the faculty in American universities. It is tempting to attribute this to their legal position. Indeed, this is the conventional explanation. Yet the legal supremacy of the administration is of recent date and represents more the acknowledgment of triumph than the source of it. Unquestionably, the administration makes good use of its legal prerogative, but there seems little doubt that its supremacy could be maintained without such aid.

For the administration reaps the benefit of what is a virtual monopoly status in respect to the faculty. A faculty member seeking position elsewhere is likely to obtain one only with the approval of the administration of the new institution. While the administration does not everywhere select the faculty, it will have, almost everywhere, the right of veto. Should there be any doubt of his cooperativeness, the new administration will check with its counterpart. This does not mean that a faculty member involved in a fracas with his administration has no place to go. If he has not been fired, his administration may be as desirous of his leaving as he is and feel no scruples in deceiving his prospective employer. The new employer, however, may check back through several past institutions, who will not be similarly motivated to conceal the facts. A professor, having had one scrape with authority, is constrained to be doubly cautious.

A professor is not, of course, required to remain in the educational enclave. While classicists or professors of English literature will find scant uses for their talents outside the educational system, many professors have no such handicaps. The professor who enjoys the comfort of knowing he has a safe retreat may be more outspoken in his relationships, but from the point of view of the system, it will make little difference. Sooner or later, such a one will have his bluff called. Once outside the system, he is likely to remain, perforce, outside. The larger the number of professors with the option of moving outside who actually withdraw from the system, the more dependent and pliable the remaining faculty becomes.

Administrative officers, per contra, are not handicapped in future occupational prospects by poor relations with faculty. An institution is likely to consider a candidate rather the better than the worse for some repute of firmness.

The situation, then, tends to be progressive. The mere removal of those faculty members best situated to exercise leadership reduces the effectiveness of the faculty in its power struggle with the administration. This gives the administration greater voice in the selection of faculty members, which voice is used to exile more incipient leaders.

Still, while such a condition accounts for the ability of the administration to consolidate its position, it does not suffice to explain the origin of administrative preeminence.

The decisive power of the administration would seem, rather, to arise from its position astride the channels by which the institution receives money. In private institutions, the outstanding source of revenue is the benevolence of wealthy persons, living and dead. It is in large measure the duty of the more important members of the administration to solicit gifts for the institution on the basis of personal popularity and with such aid as the governmental procedures for taxation provide. While some of the contacts maintained by the president—for it is upon this worthy that the bulk of the onus falls—are of such a personal nature as to suggest they will shrivel away in his absence, others—most notably gifts from those already deceased—can be considered as negotiable. The president would be somewhat less than human if he failed to take some advantage of a position where, if he is even moderately successful, he will be considered indispensable.

Further, it is not to be expected that large sums of money are to be donated without some expectation on the part of the donor that steps will be taken to remedy what he may consider intolerable abuses. It is endemic to the process of education that every man considers himself able to prescribe remedies for the ills, real and imaginary, which beset it. For every man is convinced that he has the makings of an educator, just as he has the makings of a detective. As a result, the president is unable, for the most part, to collect the amounts of money that school pride, not to mention the institution's creditors, demand without making some substantive concessions. These concessions are, for the most part, given verbally, and the institution is, to a large degree, dependent upon the president's report of the implicit and explicit commitments the institution has acquired along with its revenue. Since the president will have opinions of his own about running the institution, which opinions he will be at some pains to implement, opponents of the president's policy are constantly faced with the possibility that their own preferences menace not only the level of education but also the financial condition of the institution. The president is not highly motivated, then, to make explicit which policies follow from the financial exigencies of the situation and which flow from the president's own conception of the ideal institution, even if he has taken the trouble to separate these categories in his own mind. It is too marked a convenience for an administrator to have the option of naming others as the authors of unpopular policies and oneself as the author of popular ones.

Lest this explanation seem too pat or too local, it may be apropos to digress to consider that similar situations occur regularly in the marketing of intangibles. It is a matter of common notoriety in the advertising world that policies within an advertising agency are determined by the sales force. Such other prerogatives of power as large salaries, titles, and corner offices fall naturally to those through whom the revenue is channeled. In social and market research, when those most intangible commodities, facts, are purported to be sold, a similar situation exists.

In public institutions, the situation differs slightly. It is not private philanthropists who must be brought to that highly unnatural state in which a man is willing to part with money, but public officials, whose generosity is given a wider scope by virtue of the fact that the monies dispersed are not their own. High administrative posts in public institutions are political appointments, and it is the usual case that they are given to those with some diplomatic skill in attracting the favors of those potentates in a position to make decisions for the body politic. The president of an institution, having been appointed by virtue of abilities in negotiating with those sectors of the outside society that provide support and helpful advice to public institutions, does not find these abilities any less in demand after his appointment. His continued good relations with decision makers in the society give him an indispensability comparable to that of the president of a private institution. Nor are the faculties of public institutions in possession of any more information than their private counterparts regarding the commitments the institution is required to make.

The strategic positions enjoyed by presidents and deans are, to a surprising degree, capitalized on by lesser administrative officers. These are the creatures of the high administrative officers as the faculty are not. However well-intentioned the president may be, he cannot carry on all the authoritative function of the institution by himself. He wants a bureaucracy, preferably one loyal to him. It is a matter of common knowledge that the most efficacious way of insuring the loyalty of colleagues is to see to it that they hold office by your leave. In any struggle, then, between lesser administrative officers and faculty, the president is likely to have good reason to side with the former. The administration has, therefore, a degree of common interest less conspicuous among the faculty.

In general, it can be assumed that those groups who are able to function as units have an advantage, *ceteris paribus,* over those unable to so function. The administration tends to be numerically smaller—though it would be presumptuous to assume that such a situation must be continued indefinitely—is constructed in a more rigidly hierarchical fashion, enjoys a communion of fate that the faculty does not, and, for the moment at least, sees its own future as bound to the particular institution rather than to the field.

The lower levels of administration, however, have more at stake in their power relationship with the faculty than approbation. An administrator is expected to keep his department running smoothly. A quiescent faculty is part of his job. Thus, his relationships with the faculty form part of his professional task, while for the faculty member the relationship is largely a personal matter. Faculty members differ in the way in which they define their jobs and, obviously, some of them see certain actions of the administration as impinging on the faculty's sphere of professional competence. Nevertheless, even this overlap is seen as peripheral, while the issue is seen as central to the administrator. While this may present the administration with only the smallest of advantages in a single case, over a protracted period of time, the professionalization of the administration in this area may be decisive.

As part of their professional prerogative of concern with this area, administrators have access to information that is available to the faculty members later, if at all. Here, again, any single datum is unlikely to be decisive, but the general advantage will tell in the long run.

Further, the administration is strengthened by the tendency of leadership to gravitate to administrative posts. The faculty must be expected periodically to develop members with an interest in and a talent for political battle. On occasion, these can be expected to return like Cincinnatus to the plow. But those who achieve some success in the process of arguing some cause are likely to find that procedure exhilarating. Those with a taste for administration can easily be absorbed into the cadres of administrative offices, where their abilities at persuasion or coercion have full sway, unhampered by the demands of lecturing or prestige accumulation.

The faculty is then in the position of periodically suffering the loss of leadership to the outside world in the case of defeat and to the administration in the case of success. The administration suffers from no comparable attrition. Some administrative officers may find positions outside the educational enclave, or even turn to academic life, but the numbers of such are not a severe handicap.

Finally, the administration has the advantage of choosing the conditions under which it will announce changes. If there is a possibility of a battle, the administration can usually have its choice of time and place. It is not unusual for controversial policies to be announced, for example, in May. The school year being virtually ended, there is little time to organize opposition. Faculty members, immersed in the wistful perusal of travel brochures, railroad schedules, and student examinations, are in no mood for political infighting. As in the closing hours of a legislative session, much can be accomplished at this time that would otherwise be hindered by calm appraisal.

The summer months also provide an advantageous time for the promulgation of directives whose reception would be, in other circumstances, dubious. The faculty, dispersed hither and yon, returns to a *fait accompli*. The initiative has been lost.

Despite this formidable list of faculty disadvantages, the faculty is not without some influence when united. This last condition is the rub. The faculty is likely to unite for few causes, with the possible exception of increased faculty salaries. Competition is endemic among faculties, and prolonged and rancorous enmity between colleagues is common enough to occasion no surprise. A professor with a large psychological and intellectual investment in his opposition to one of his fellows is unlikely to surrender this for petty or transient causes. It is only matters of weight and import that will override the Balkan atmosphere that pervades the campus.

Needless to say, administrators are nothing loath to deal with faculty members on an individual basis. There is, from the point of view of the administration, no need to consider as matters of principle the details of negotiations conducted by the administration with some single member. It is even, at times, to the advantage of the member to deal in private with matters that might otherwise be considered public policy. It is only over a larger range of activities that the house never loses.

The ability to judge each case in terms of its own pressures and advantages—the technical term is on its merits—is of immense tactical advantage. It prevents a development of equities or precedence that will curb the actions of authorities. A system of collective bargaining, as employers have learned to their dismay, may generate tendencies to expand the scope of decisions which fall into its purview. Dealing on an individual basis not only places the authority at an advantage, for he may be quite willing to forego this advantage in any particular instance, but keeps in check any tendencies for the persons with whom the administration deals to find common interests and make common cause.

On those issues, however, where the faculty does choose to make a common stand, its claims to prestige stand it in good stead. Newspaper editors are likely to listen with some respect to the voice of a united faculty, perhaps the more so as it is so rare. Administrators are sensitive to the necessity of maintaining institutional prestige and ordinarily go to some lengths to prevent unfavorable publicity where an appeal to the school spirit or the faculty fails. Faculty victories do occur. It is rather the rule that faculty leaders suffer some subsequent consequences, but the faculty as a whole is not punished. On the whole, however, the administration enjoys the preeminent position.

While relationships of administration and faculty and of administration and students may take place on a group basis, or individually, relations between faculty and students are conducted largely on an individual basis. Nevertheless, the tenor of the relationships flows from the advantages of the groups involved and from group aspirations. The faculty regards itself as associated with the administration in the exercise of authority and thereby entitled to a superordinate role vis-à-vis students. The basis for these beliefs is historical. As we have seen, the faculty enjoys a position in relation to the administration markedly at variance with its conception of equity and would fain assert the authority over the students that it cannot exercise over the administration. In the past, faculty has wielded such power on the students, based on its ability to judge whether the students had fulfilled the price of the educational bargain or a specific segment thereof. This power still formally exists. Diplomas are, in theory, awarded by the unanimous consent of the faculty. Marks, as indications of the consummation of specific subbargains, are still given by faculty members. But the option that these once represented is no longer present. Award of diplomas is a rubber stamp.

The effectual abrogation of the faculty veto power has flowed from the economic situation of the institution. Production for the mass market requires a large volume which is not subject to the whims of large numbers of intermediaries. While students may be expelled for political reasons, they will not be removed for the sake of the authority of the faculty. It is uneconomical and irrational for the university to have its production dependent upon the necessity for each student to meet some series of capricious requirements. Instead, requirements are formalized, and students able to meet such formalities as the prestige of the institution requires are prima facie in good standing. While this rationalization has stood the institution in good stead, in reducing what would otherwise be a formidable attrition rate, it has not made the life of the faculty comfortable. Where faculty members may or may not be aware of the degree to which their authority is titular—the amount of unawareness may be taken as a tribute to the indomitableness of the human spirit—the students rarely fail to appraise the situation correctly.

It must be remembered that the students have a motivation to adopt mini-max procedures that is not comparable to any possessed by the faculty. While an individual faculty member may be highly interested in asserting his authority, the faculty as a whole seeks its goals in other areas.

Of course, where a faculty member objects to a specific student, he may well be successful in having him expelled. But he cannot, by the economic necessities of the institution, take such action against large numbers as would be necessary to change the relationship between professor and student.

Where the source of conflict is one of the mini-max procedures, as it commonly is, the faculty sooner or later comes face to face with the advantages to the institution of cooperation with student minimization.

Attempts by the faculty to assert authority by obstruction of the completion of educational bargains, then, end in leaving the professor the alternatives of continuing his campaign at the cost of his popularity or resigning himself to what he is likely to describe as the sad state of American education. Faculty members are likely to make this putative sad state a favorite topic of conversation and are fulsome in their descriptions of it among themselves, if somewhat more reluctant to commit themselves to print.

Nevertheless, if the faculty does not generally have ultimate power over the students, neither do the students hold any ultimate power over the faculty. The relationship will be determined, then, by less conclusive weapons. After all, few relationships proceed to the final analysis. In most instances, both sides are aware of what final results would be and prefer to stop somewhat short of the ultimate. The absence in faculty-student relationships of an inevitable result makes less difference than might at first be imagined.

Relations in a specific instance are likely to be determined by the theory of nuisance value. Where neither party has the power to control the other, the party who is able to prove more a nuisance to the other than the other is to him, is likely to have his way. The theory of nuisance value is, in essence, the theory of unrequited damage on a smaller scale. Since, by the distribution of power within the institution, faculty and students are able to do little damage to one another and can be of little benefit to each other, the scale of interrelations is reduced to that level at which they can be either pleasant or unpleasant associates. For any kind of association, one or both partners is required to forego, willingly or unwillingly, some of what would otherwise be his preferences in order to maintain the pleasantness of association. Where one of the partners has the power to inconvenience the other seriously, the latter is likely to have to do the lion's share of the foregoing. Where neither partner has any real power over the other, the degree to which a partner is willing or able to be difficult is likely to be the degree to which his associates will restrain their desires to allow play to his.

In the faculty-student relationship, both sides possess sources of nuisance value. If the professor cannot, in most instances, nullify the educational bargain, he can, to a degree, render its completion difficult and extend its duration. In many instances it is easier for the student to comply with the professorial request than to challenge it, even where the challenge might prove ultimately successful. It is rarely clear at what point a faculty member's request will become more burdensome than the nuisance of challenging it or of foregoing the subbargain will warrant, and the faculty may be the beneficiary of the doubt. However, it is unlikely that the faculty will be able to maintain acceptance of its requests far beyond its power to retaliate for any protracted period of time.

Students also possess some nuisance value. When a professor has, to their way of thinking, exceeded the number or difficulty of requests which the situation warrants, they may adopt a variety of alternatives. For the present, they may simply fail to comply. For the future, they may avoid contact with the professor, alerting others to the hazards of enrollment in his lectures. It is rare that the prospect of a seriously decreased enrollment does not dispose a professor to some degree of compromise.

Nor are students unwilling to resort to personal remonstrance or to heckling. This is the equivalent to the personal exhortation or browbeating that faculty members occasionally indulge in. Success in either case depends on the specific situation. While none of these methods are likely to prove invariably successful, limited goals are often attained where conditions are favorable.

Over a period, some degree of equilibrium is found. Professors, with experience, are likely to be able to gauge how far they can go, though new recruits must often be shown their places. The students' comparative unfamiliarity with the situation is to some degree compensated by the tendency of students to pool information and evaluations. Pitched battles are therefore less frequent than might be guessed from the ambiguities of the situation.

The foregoing analysis of faculty-student relations has been limited to the results of conflict between the groups. Yet the groups would seem to have much greater advantages from co-operation with each other in achieving greater control of their own activities at the expense of the administration. In general, the preferred strategy for the weaker members of a three-man game is to combine against the strongest. Why, then, has such a natural alliance not taken place?

The faculty member, as we have seen, has certain peculiar working conditions. The unusual absence of supervision and lack of agreement on the nature of the faculty member's job tend to threaten his prestige. Since the prestige of the faculty member is part of the bargain of education, the threat, even if it is only in the mind of the professor, is doubly serious. The faculty member is, then, under some constraint to maintain his distance from the students. An alliance with the students, however expedient, poses problems to the faculty that it does not to the students. The students will be ill disposed to form an alliance under any terms but those of equality. Students tend to have little appreciation of the difficulty of faculty members and rarely attain the flexibility that would enable them to join forces with the faculty under such conditions as the faculty would find necessary.

Naturally, the administration is not likely to encourage an alliance so fraught with the possibilities of disadvantage. The administrative policy of recognizing faculty claims to prestige, which is highly rational as a means of promoting institutional prestige, serves also to maintain the distance between faculty and student which is conducive to smooth administrative control.

Faculty-student cooperation will then be unlikely until such time as the condition of the faculty has changed so far for the worse that radical revision of the faculty frame of reference is necessary.

10

The Effects of Other Enclaves

For the purposes of simplicity, we have considered education simply as a bargain entered into for the sake of prestige. On this basis, we have attempted to set up a model, sketching out the implications for educational institutions that would follow from such a hypothesis. The time has come to complicate the model a bit.

We have assumed that prestige is common currency, equally negotiable in any group. Actually, this is far from the case. The value of a Ph.D. in psychology is negligible for an aspiring chemist; a future psychologist will have as little use for a diploma in chemistry. Advancement in a profession generally requires prestige of a specialized kind. There are some occupations, for the most part recently developed specialties, that recognize several kinds of diplomas, but by and large it can be said that most trades acknowledge only prestige required in their own specialties.

This being the case, it might have been more logical to view an educational institution as a parallel series of institutions that happen to utilize common facilities. To some extent, such an approach can be justified. Students intending to enter a particular occupation will respond to changes in the employment situation of that occupation. Various fads and fancies in the educational program will follow, howbeit tardily, the fashions in the occupation. Nonetheless, an educational institution does possess a unity that pervades the various departments, even when they disagree most profoundly.

Furthermore, the various occupations are not as dissimilar as some of the more partisan advocates would contend. The occupations of the Western world have tended to follow a common pattern, picking up styles from one another. While the speeds at which the different occupations have developed have varied, the general direction of development has not. Increasingly, occupations have tended to share certain characteristics.

In the last half-century, the drive of the occupations has been toward professionalization. Not all occupations have come to resemble the archetypes, but virtually all have moved in that direction. By tradition, the oldest professions have been characterized by a strong professional society, rigorous control of entrants, a code of ethics, the prohibition of practice by unlicensed practitioners, and the stress on the client-professional relationship. Virtually all of the facets of professional practice have, in the case of medicine and law, been operative before modern times. It is only in the last fifty years, however, that the attempt on the part of other trades to copy them has been widespread.

The attempt, however, has met with differential success. With the rise of the nation-state, the power to make such professional claims stick resides with the State. It follows that all would-be professions turn to some form of lobbying to carry out the more ambitious parts of their programs. Thus far, legislatures have been cool. With some few exceptions, they have demanded that associations show good cause for the State to interfere with the free play of the marketplace to the benefit of the associations. Not that the State has been loath to interfere in economic matters. It has, however, been chary of delegating its powers to nongovernmental bodies. In this respect its policy has been rational. Nongovernmental bodies do not provide jobs for political supporters.

Whatever the grounds for the comparative coolness of the State's attitude, prospective professions have had to turn to other avenues. The formation of associations has presented no problem; they abound. The drawing up of codes of ethics, lists of standards of the profession, and guides to the proper relationship with clients, co-workers, and professionals in allied fields have followed hard thereon. Wherever there is a will, it is a question of time before these codes are completed, if provisional. Interests are balanced, concessions are made to denigrate behaviors that have been begun before the formation of the association, and a standard is raised to which the majority of the profession can repair.

However, there are dissidents. Some public opinion, both inside and outside the organization, must be brought to bear. Economic sanctions are considered; on occasion, they are even tried. An educational campaign is undertaken. In general, the newer professional associations have not met with outstanding success in their attempts to monopolize their fields (the technical term is raising standards). They have not had legal backing; they have hesitated to employ force; they have not enjoyed the support of public opinion. In large measure, they have suffered from the internal contradictions of their position; they have desired the benefits of unionization without the loss of dignity. This approach has in some respects resembled the efforts of the craft unions. They have endeavored to gain their ends as gentlemen, yet their specialized base has prevented the lay world from feeling the sympathy of kinship. The layman, lacking the feeling that he might some day be a professional himself, has not joined in the effort to strengthen the professional's hand.

The associations have not been without some victories. If they have failed to persuade present practitioners to desist from various dubieties, they have been able to make common cause with the dissidents to restrict future entry. As the path of least resistance the setting of qualifications for future entrance has attained widespread approval. In most cases, these qualifications are educational. Where no attempt is made to hinder the activities of those presently in the field, all may join in requiring future competition to meet standards.

The choice of educational qualifications has been felicitous. First, any qualification reduces the number of entrants. Since the potential revenue is considered as a relatively fixed quantity, the reduction of the number of persons enjoying the benefits yields a larger share to those fortunate enough to have gotten an early start. Second, even for those who do manage to enter, the necessity of the diploma postpones their competitive activities for a number of years. Further, since education costs money, the qualification restricts entrants to persons from higher income families, in the terms in which the debate is usually couched, a finer class of people. Insofar as this change tends to yield a group with greater prestige, the benefits of increased status are enjoyed also by the earlier arrivals. On several counts, then, the setting of educational requirements recommends itself to professional societies as a means of advancing the status of the occupation.

While the reasons given above are by no means covert, the primary justification for this approach has been in terms of the acquisition of requisite knowledge. The discussion has generally assumed that education is directed to the amassing of knowledge and that the possession of the diploma is a guarantee of the successful acquisition of certain specified data and skills. The assumption has rarely been questioned despite the almost constant flow of criticism claiming that graduates of educational institutions do not, in fact, possess the data and skills that they are purported to be amassing. Let us then look more carefully into the question of the relationship of knowledge and education.

Knowledge tends to grow progressively.[1] This can be expected in any open society. Each person has available to him the results of his predecessors' endeavors. He can avoid blind alleys and concentrate on more likely possibilities. As a result, each generation can advance beyond its predecessor.

This is not an inevitable development; it is a possibility. For example, the late Middle Ages saw consistent expansion of philosophy and theology. Several hundred years of development left even mediocre philosophers able to argue with considerably more subtlety in these areas than the ancients and able to recognize the consequences of various positions taken by the Greeks which previous ages were obviously unaware of. On the other hand, farming showed no such consistent development. In the vast majority of cases farmers pursued their occupation exactly as their fathers and grandfathers did.

Nor can this elaboration be contributed to the effect of science. Theology has shown this expansion on the basis of logic; shamanism, on the basis of empiricism; and literary criticism, on the basis of aesthetics. It is not necessary to the development of a field of thought to have hardware.

Perhaps the difference can be attributed to the effects of competition. For example, the level of abilities of chess players rises from generation to generation, masters being loath to accord status to any less skilled than themselves. Third-rate chess players will often be more skilled than the first-rate players of a century earlier.

In any event, knowledge in a particular profession can easily reach a point where it cannot be absorbed by a single individual. This presents a problem to the practitioner. Where it is possible in theory to learn all there is to know about a profession, the question of training is academic. A novice must learn everything. When this is no longer possible, different members of the same profession can no longer be presumed to be able to communicate. The usual answer to this problem has been to specialize. Presumably a core of common knowledge remains. As the process gains momentum, however, even this may not be true. For a while after the event, lip service is still paid to the old ideals by which any member of the profession could do any job given to the professional. In practice, newcomers get training on the job in the particular knowledge they need.

From the point of view of knowledge, then, the ideal situation for learning is that of an apprentice in the firm in which he will be employed. However felicitous this approach may be, viewed in terms of quantity and appropriateness of knowledge gained, it conflicts with the prestige requirements of the profession. In order for occupations to claim status in the community, they wish to admit candidates previously prestiged by education. As a result of these conflicing requirements of professional life, then, neophytes must be educated in institutions and receive the knowledge of professional matters subsequently on the job.

The awareness that professionals are, in fact, being trained on the job will, of course, filter back to candidates still in educational institutions. These will then be in a position to assess realistically the value of the knowledge that it is possible to acquire in the institution.

While this is the practice, the theory, of course, deviates. Since it is necessary to justify the setting of educational requirements, it must be maintained that the purpose of education is the acquisition of knowledge. Educational institutions are, therefore, formally given the job of fostering the growth of professional knowledge.

This, indeed, would be a formidable task. Given a profession whose principles are in a state of flux—and most professions could be so characterized today—whose activities grow constantly more diverse, and whose discoveries tomorrow are unpredictable today, how can the institution prepare neophytes for professional positions? Obviously, from the point of view of knowledge, educational institutions are singularly ill-equipped. A career in the educational enclave is not likely to acquaint one with the state of professional knowledge.

Where, then, is the institution to get the knowledge to convey to its students? Even if we assume that some practitioners have acquired familiarity with sufficient specialties of the profession to have a general overview, and to follow development in the field through professional connections and through careful perusal of the literature, such men are unlikely to leave their jobs to join the faculty. If an institution is fortunate enough to acquire such a man, several years of faculty work should suffice to reduce his contacts with his profession to the point where he is no longer in touch with the field. In terms of propagating knowledge, the solution might be for institutions to employ the part-time services of professionals actively in practice. This policy, however, fails to give the institution the required prestige.

Of necessity, then, the institution experiences a lag between the genesis of professional developments and the time when the news of them reaches the faculty, since the faculty is recruited largely from those not actively in practice. While the exact state of the profession is not known to the students, they are often aware of the difference between professional matters as taught in the schools and as practiced.

Institutions in general are left with two alternatives. They can propagate the techniques of the profession available to them, ignoring the gap between the profession as learned by the professors and as presently carried out, or they can attempt to teach general principles, relying on postinstitutional apprenticeship to propagate technical knowledge. Neither of these alternatives is without disadvantages.

The technical solution does gain the institution the opportunity to discuss a vast amount of data. In those professions that use mechanical aids, it justifies the acquisition of much expensive and space-consuming hardware. While the cost of this is a drawback to the institution, hardware does have high visibility. It conduces to the image of the university as sincere and up-to-date. Moreover, even the disbursement of money may, on occasion, be put to some use in an economical institution. The purchase of particularly expensive hardware may be made the keynote of requests for funds, in the expectation that the appeal of the concrete will result in receiving more money than required for its purchase. Nor is the expectation disappointed.

Using the technical approach, the institution can set up a large number of subbargains, provide an appealing catalogue, and consider itself in the forefront of progress. The rub is provided by the fact that techniques in modern society are far more perishable than general principles. Hardware, probably subject to temporal lag at the time of installation, rapidly becomes obsolete. In a society in which technical equipment in use in the field is often obsolete before it has begun to wear out, the institution cannot hope to compete. Further, insofar as the students have absorbed the techniques used as a basis for discussion in the institution, they will have to unlearn them on the job. Students of technical schools who have cooperated too heartily with the institution's program will be at a disadvantage compared to students from more theoretical schools.

The theoretical alternative, too, has its disadvantages. The students will have less erroneous data to contend with but, from an institutional point of view—an attitude that the administration is at some pains to adopt—the theoretical approach offers less advantages. It is possible to maintain the appearance of conveying equal amounts of information, while avoiding technical questions. This does present some strain to all but the most experienced professors, however. Students may feel ill equipped for professional work, and their nervousness is contagious. In institutions of this nature, the usual response is to accent the academic nature of the institution. The separation from the world inherent in this approach is presented as an advantage, the student's last opportunity to think constructively before plunging into the whirl of work.

Even theory, however, is not immune to obsolescence. While its life is longer than that of technique, even its position in a fast-moving society is transitory. Its passing, however, does not take place in the institution in peace. When professors have committed themselves to a particular theoretical approach, they are likely to have a larger stake in their opinions than their more technically-minded brethren have in theirs. They will be at some pains to defend the old theory, occasionally even beyond the point where it can be considered objectively defensible. When this occurs, the institutional position may become that of the backwaters of the profession and serve to alienate the institution from its professional base, to some degree. The theoretical alternative then enjoys the short-range advantage of less expense and less frequent obsolescence and the long-range disadvantage of generating greater difficulties when theory changes.

Given, then, the alternative of theoretical or technical approach, what is the rational student's response? For the moment, we will assume that the student has full knowledge of the general situation of the profession that he plans to enter. At first blush, he appears confronted with the dilemma. In order to enter his profession, he must have a diploma. To acquire the diploma, he must give some indication of having absorbed various information. This information, however, is largely a disadvantage in the profession if it is technical and irrelevant if it is theoretical. Furthermore, to advance in his profession, he may desire to begin acquisition of the intellectual tools of his trade immediately. These are available to him insofar as he is employed in his profession or insofar as the information is in print. Time is at a premium, however, and the time-meeting institutional requirements delay the acquisition of professional skills.

In fact, the student is not nearly as helpless as first impressions would indicate. He may adopt a mini-max procedure toward his educational responsibilities. The resulting freeing of time can be devoted, if desired, to professional advancement. We may expect, then, that the student most committed to advancement in his field and most aware of the professional scene will be among those most highly motivated to pursue mini-max procedures. Insofar as educational activities are concerned, his behavior will not differ markedly from the student who adopts mini-max procedures to free his time for leisure, for an avocation, or in the pursuit of general knowledge.

What, however, of the student who lacks the information on the state of the profession for which he is a candidate? During the course of education, he is likely to hear something of the state of affairs, a favorite topic of conversation in educational institutions. He has not yet had these opportunities when he enters, however. He may be seen as beginning, in the absence of any information, with the simplifying assumption that the picture of the profession that emerges from his lectures represents its actual condition. If this were the case, rational behavior would require that he absorb as much information as can be garnered in the course of his lectures. This is a limiting case, where the dictates of rational behavior approach the standard educational model.

It is not necessary to go into great detail about how the conventional model of the good student works. This ideal type has been drawn in great length by many learned educators who, while they disagree in details, agree in general outline. Their picture, however, while not reproduced in detail either, is an integral part of the economic model drawn up in this study. It is the rational approach to education of a student in the complete absence of information about the state of affairs in the field he is entering.

To what extent any appreciable part of the student population approaches this limiting case is difficult to say. Certainly, the proportion does not resemble that predicted by exponents of the theory. Western culture is something of an open society, and all sorts of information are to hand for those interested in its acquisition. The insulation of educational institutions varies greatly. In even the most secluded academic atmosphere, some data on the professional situation can be assumed to seep in. Of course, a student who has operated in the absence of data for a protracted period of time may have acquired an emotional investment in his behavior and may maintain irrational responses for some greater or lesser amount of time. To the extent that such irrationality occurs, it will appear to confirm the assumptions of standard educational theory.

In any event, the degree of information available is a question for empirical research. The model presented has predicated behavior under conditions of full information and of no information in regard to any particular subbargain at the institution. A fuller treatment than is here envisaged would take into account quanta of information on professional matters and could, in all probability, predict patterns of rational action for varying circumstances of partial information. This task, however, we will leave to future investigators.

The question of the occupational relationship to education, however, should not be closed without a further word on the present situation of on-the-job training. Until the 1940s most on-the-job training was largely informal. Of late, it has become far more institutional and has begun to lay down more formal requirements, patterned to a large degree on existing educational institutions. The comparatively specialized nature of this training has restricted the negotiability of the prestige acquired in these post-institutional proceedings. It would be presumptuous to assume that this will be an insurmountable barrier to the development of on-the-job training into a full-fledged educational institution. It must be remembered that the diplomas of educational institutions are, to a large extent, negotiable only within a single occupation. Nor has this limitation prevented the development of these institutions. The future may see the present pattern of education extended several years further. The exact nature of such post-institutional institutions cannot be predicted at this point. But an assumption that they will show much of the dynamic interaction of present institutions would not be amiss.

11

The Status of Standard
Educational Theory

This work has focused largely on an attempt to explain practices in the educational enclave. Except for a brief discussion of standard educational theory in the first chapter and some subsequent passing references to its inadequacy for explaining certain educational practices, I have not given much consideration to what is, in fact, the usual set of concepts for understanding the enclave. I would like to pay some attention to the status of standard educational theory before concluding this present volume. Let us begin by considering the major differences between standard educational theory and the theory of coercive bargaining as here applied to the educational enclave.

Standard educational theory considers the transmission of education as the essence of activity in education; this volume considers the essence to be the certification of prestige. Perhaps the strongest argument against considering information the nexus of

educational activity is the fact that virtually all educational theorists agree that the amount of information transmitted by educational institutions is substantially below the amount to be
expected on the basis of educational theory. That most of the
experts consider this divergence an unhappy historical accident
remediable by tightening a few bolts here and there in the educational machinery is more a tribute to their optimism than to
the logic of their position. In fact, the amount of data transmitted by educational institutions is minimal and much of that,
misleading.

The selection of prestige as the crucial good dealt with in the
educational enclave is not an automatic deduction from the
theory of coercive bargaining. That theory merely suggests that
education forms an enclave whose regularities flow from government strategy and whose interactions may be understood in
terms of bargaining which begins with economic considerations
and may escalate into the power dimension. One could, with
complete logical consistency, develop an explanation of education compatible with the theory of coercive bargaining based on
the assumption that the good that was being bargained for was
information. Educational institutions would sell information
and students would buy it. The bargaining would follow the
general principles laid down by the theory's notion of the kind of
coercive bargaining that is normal for human interaction.

My selection of prestige as the essential element was primarily
based on empiric observation of the educational scene without
the lenses of educational theory. A cursory review of the historical situation suggests that educational institutions severed the
connection between granting prestige tokens and transmitting
information in the early Middle Ages before the foundations for
modern educational institutions were properly laid.

Understanding education in terms of prestige has the advantage of locating educational institutions functionally in the
modern world. While the modern world makes some use of information, it does so nowhere in the quantities that would serve to
justify the vast apparatus of the educational enclave. What information is used is generally developed in business or govern-

mental enterprises and is the work of a comparatively small number of experts. The vast majority of citizens make as little use of information as in any other time in history. On the other hand, the modern world has replaced the comparatively rigid social-class distinctions that characterized earlier societies by a social continuum based largely upon prestige. This change has encouraged the growth of educational institutions and, in turn, been made possible by this growth. The selection of prestige as the key concept for understanding education thus contributes to the development of an explanation that integrates education into the body of sociological knowledge respecting the modern world.

Standard educational theory treats education as a process; the theory of coercive bargaining treats it as a series of transactions. While there are certain human interactions which, for the present, can realistically be treated only in terms of process, the modern trend is toward using the concept of transaction. The essential difficulty with process-type explanations is the inability to establish any clear points in the analysis. Although such an explanation can be justified for the description of interactions which empirically show no beginning, ending, or change points, modern education scarcely seems to fit this description. Collegiate education has a fixed date for starting and terminating. The position of any student is readily calculable in terms of the number of subbargains successfully concluded. There seems to be no a priori reason for considering education as resistant to a transactional explanation. A transactional explanation, similarly, has the advantage that it is possible to borrow from the fund of transactional concepts that have been developed during the last four hundred years. There seems little question that the state of transactional theory is far more developed than that of process theory.

Standard educational theory assumes that the motivation of at least one of the partners to education is altruistic; the theory of coercive bargaining assumes that all partners bargain in terms of maximizing their self-interest. Ultimately, assertions of basic motivation cannot be proved or disproved, but it is of historical interest that all noneducational theories since the late Middle Ages have shifted from the assumption of altruism on the part of the individual to the assumption of self-interest. This does not constitute a rebuttal to the defenders of standard educational theory, but it does put them in the position of either arguing that people's behavior in the educational enclave is substantially different from the behavior of what is often the same people outside the educational enclave or that the rest of social science has gone fundamentally astray. In either event, they are hard put to link their explanations to explanations of what is happening in the rest of the world.

As a corollary of the postulated motivations, standard economic theory assumes the motivations of both partners to the educational endeavor to be fundamentally in agreement; the theory of coercive bargaining believes their interests opposed as far as the appropriate point of the bargain, although sufficiently compatible so that a bargain is mutually profitable. Were the standard educational theorists correct, the campus should be a scene of idyllic harmony. This does not seem to be the case.

All of these comparisons and criticisms, if they are to be taken seriously, provide us with an enigma. Standard educational theory appears to differ fundamentally from other theories in the social sciences. It takes, as starting points, assumptions that all other fields of the social sciences have long since abandoned. It uses styles of explanations accepted by other social sciences only as a last resort. Its explanations fail to dovetail with the explanations current in any other field. It is, in short, a complete historical anomaly.

Nor, for that matter, do its explanations fit its own history. They are better suited to the Greek schools of philosophy of two millennia ago than to any of the educational institutions in the intervening time.

The problem, then, is how standard educational theory has managed to survive vicissitudes of thought that have beset every other theory. In every other field the theories of even fifty years ago are antiquarian curiosities. Standard educational theory marches on, seemingly, like the Deacon's one-horse shay, oblivious to the ravages of time.

The answer, of course, is that we have been analyzing theory in purely logical terms. The successive theories in the social sciences are not contingent on their logical purity. If we are to understand the status of standard educational theory, we must attempt a functional analysis.

We may begin with the basic notion that the function of theory is the legitimation of behavior. The notion thus simply expressed has ramifications. Theory legitimates not only past behavior, but also present and future behavior. But if certain future behaviors are legitimated, while alternate behaviors are denied the benefit of legitimation, theory will serve to promote certain actions at the expense of others. But even as the theory advances the cause of certain behaviors, it is in turn dependent upon them. Only if the behavior legitimated occurs is the theory validated. The divine right of kings, in the absence of kings, becomes a historical curiosity.

The formulation raises some difficulties, however. The notion that the function of theory is to legitimate behavior is itself a theory, however rudimentary. Accordingly, it should legitimate some behavior. But it does not. It is a simple exposition. If the notion is correct, it should not exist. We are now in the world of the Spanish barber and the Russell set.

We might then consider a Russell type of solution. The sociology of knowledge is not a theory, but a metatheory: a theory about theories. While theories$_1$ must be promotional, legitimizing some behavior, theories$_2$, metatheories, may be expository. After all, metatheories can be considered the province of experts; they are practically semantics.

Alas, expository theory will not stay under the carpet. Djilas simultaneously made the best-seller lists and the antisocial register with the theory that is clearly expository.[1] There are others.

The artless simplicities of our notion will have to be curbed. We shall have to recognize the existence of two types of theory, promotional and expository.

The expository theory is easier to deal with. It is designed to explain phenomena. Insofar as it correctly postdicts and predicts action, it is entitled to attention. In competition with other theories, it may fail to account for enough phenomena, may require too many assumptions, may be internally inconsistent, or may be inconsistent with a solidly based explanation for other phenomena; any of these defects can be held against it. Basically, it falls if it fails to account in an elegant fashion for the way things are. Generally, the expository theory, even if it cannot be refuted, will not attain a mass following. Its enjoyment is likely to be confined to isolated scholastic enclaves. It will boast few defenders in the court of popular appeal, for there are few who stand to benefit from its popularity. Its standing is a matter of academic interest.

Mannheim's notion of the sociology of knowledge might be seen as an expository theory.[2] Mannheim seems to visualize the theory as the first of a series by the free intelligentsia, a new class. But the free intelligentsia has not developed. It may be more parsimonious to assume that expository theories may be developed by individuals and may not attain a large following in the absence of a group whose interests coincide with the theorist's.

The promotional theory, per contra, causes a stir in the real world. Every faction will have a theory to convince the wavering, disconcert the opposition, and comfort supporters. The measure of a theory's popularity, while it can be empirically ascertained, is likely to be more of an indication of the logistics of the power struggle than of the content of the theory.

Assessment of the merit of a promotional theory is more difficult. Concerned with the legitimacy of behavior, the theory applies to the realm of what ought to be. This is a shadowy region, from whose bourn men return with different maps. In theory, nothing men do or fail to do disturbs one efficacy of the argument. Here, justice may triumph though the heavens fall. One cannot evaluate by logic what ought to be.

But the notion of what should be is not made up of whole cloth. It is an extrapolation of behaviors or tendencies existing in the world as it is. Were it not so, the theory should be incomprehensible, perhaps even ineffable. Nor is the theory likely to gain support as a theory solely of what ought to be. It is precisely most effective when presented as a theory of what is. As such, its status is ambiguous. Explaining legitimate behavior, it is forced to attribute alternative behaviors to malice or perversity. If it were, in fact, to provide an impartial explanation, it would forfeit its usefulness. The degree to which it succeeds in explaining the world that is, is a result of the persuasiveness of its argument or the strength of its supporters rather than the rigor of its logic. Even when the standard applied to it is the same as to expository theory, the interpretation of the results is different.

While the distinction between promotional and expository theory is rather easily drawn, deciding the status of particular theories may be a nice exercise. The case of classical economic theory is an example.

From the point of view of explaining prices, classical economic theory is expository. Starting from the notion that parties to a bargain will act in accordance with their own best interests, the theory showed that price is the result of the desirability of the item and the difficulty of procuring it. The tendency of labor and capital to move to more profitable enterprises equalized profit in different endeavors and maintained a certain degree of stability of price. The classical economist went on to argue that the free marketplace gave society the greatest amount of economic goods. The government was urged to restrain its impulses to tamper with the machinery.

As we can see, the theory was not without its promotional aspects. The resultant benefit to the common good served to legitimize the desire of the merchant to follow his own interest, which previous theories, set up for the benefit of warriors and priests, had considered downright greedy. Although the notion that men may legitimately seek their own interest is presently taken for granted, at the time it was revolutionary. Further, the advice to the government makes sense only if we are to understand the government as altruistically devoted to the common good. In any era, this notion is promotional. In general, it is presently considered that the success of classical economic theory is due less to its charm than to the particular utility of these promotional ideas to the rising merchant class.

The triumph of classical economics was short-lived, but its successors continued to maintain that individuals followed their own interests while the state was dedicated to the pursuit of the *summum bonum*. They modified the theory only to the degree that the government's altruistic motivation was taken to require more active policies. This basic structure underlies current theory today.

Theories dealing with the production and sale of tangible goods enjoy relatively little leeway. It is passing difficult to maintain that the manufacturer of copper kettles is in business from altruistic considerations.[3] The production of intangibles, however, seems to offer wider scope. It is always something of a moot point exactly what function the intangible serves, and we may depend on the theoretician to opt that choice which places the industry in the most favorable light.

As a case in point, we may examine the theory of the press. Two hundred years ago, newspapers and periodicals, the press, existed as a vehicle by which editors expressed their viewpoints on affairs of the day, hoping to keep adherents of their own actions informed and perhaps to persuade the unconvinced and an occasional opponent. The revenue for this enterprise was derived from two sources. Purchasers' pennies went far toward covering the expense and the remaining deficit was usually taken care of by a subsidy from those who wished to have their viewpoint represented in the press.

To maintain this proceeding, the benevolence of the government was required. The freedom of the press guaranteed in the Constitution served to relieve editors of the restraints previously exercised by the fear of jail sentences or worse. The government further contributed a direct subsidy in the form of postal services sold to editors below cost. The economic margin provided by this subsidy was often crucial in a competitive market.

In the course of time, the nature of the press has changed. Predominant revenue for the press now comes from the advertisement of wares. Contributions by those of like minds are virtually unheard of. Since advertisers pay rates set in direct proportion with the size of circulation, the press has been understandably chary of increasing the cost to readers. In fact, during sales campaigns, subscribers are offered substantial discounts. The direct revenue from readers, as a rule, now provides only a small fraction of the press's budget.

From the point of view of space, the advertiser's share similarly predominates. The number of column inches which correspond to what would have been the contents of a newspaper or periodical two hundred years ago has grown correspondingly small. By any quantitative standard, therefore, today's press would have to be regarded primarily as a medium for advertising wares.

As far as the concern of the publisher goes, information is more difficult to come by. However, A. J. Liebling, an acute observer of the press, maintains that publishers would be more than happy to dispense entirely with news items and articles, could they but be assured that their competitors would adopt a similar policy.[4]

However, the consistent use of a theory of the press as an advertising medium would menace the benevolence of the government as expressed in second-class mailing privileges. The advantage offered to advertisers who make use of the post office via the press as compared with advertisers who use the post office directly forms a critical part of the press's financial structure.

The maintenance of the theory of the press as a medium for news and comment offers publishers several subsidiary benefits. It entitles a publisher to be considered as an authority on all sorts of questions public and private, to a degree which would make the manager of any other enterprise of equal size green with envy.

Of course, the current theory of the press was not specifically designed to serve these purposes. It simply resulted from the failure to take sufficient account of a gradual secular change in the structure of the press. The effectiveness of the theory does not suffer.

The advantage of dealing in intangible goods is readily apparent. The theorist has a considerably wider range of alternative explanations for the behavior of the merchant. It may be expected that that alternative will be opted which places the merchant in the most favorable light. With this in mind, we may proceed to our examination of educational theory.

We have seen that educational institutions bestow tokens of prestige. This prestige is used by the purchaser to legitimate status in the outside world. It is, therefore, a *sine qua non* of promotional educational theory that it legitimate this transaction. We have seen, also, that prestige is legitimated as a recognition of some virtue or cluster of virtues in its bearer. The educational institution takes cognizance of the prestige lineage, the actual or potential prowess, and the intellectual ability of its students. Any one of these might serve the purpose as the foundation of an educational theory. Since the theory serves best if it attracts a mass following, it is advisable that the theory not be needlessly complicated by the simultaneous consideration of more than one virtue. While each of the three possible theories meets the primary requirement of legitimizing the transaction, the various side effects make for different degrees of utility.

An educational theory by which prestige tokens would be accorded by educational institutions on the basis of the students' contact with persons of prestiged lineage requires a faculty composed at least in part of such persons. However, in a society based primarily on economic standing—we may for the moment disregard the question of whether the standing rests on the acquisition of large amounts of money or on the conspicuous spending of large amounts of money—persons of prestige are likely to have substantial incomes. They will not, then, consent to the sacrifice entailed in being a member of a faculty upon the same reasonable terms with which present faculty members are hired.

Of course, the expense of such a policy to educational institutions need not be excessive. It must be remembered that educational institutions are themselves in the business of marketing prestige. They are thus in the enviable position of using as faculty their own product, forming a closed system. Thus, the number of additional prestiged persons, that is, those whose claims to prestige arise from outside the educational system, would be minimal. Nevertheless, educational institutions perennially operate on a tight budget, and the addition of even a small added expense is looked upon with disfavor.

The formulation of an educational theory based on the notion that diplomas are granted for prowess at the tourneys is a more active contender. The changes in the role of the faculty would be considerably smaller; undoubtedly, most present members would be equally at home under such a set-up. An occasional professor confined to a wheelchair might perhaps suffer some inconvenience. It must again be remembered that the criteria for sufficient prestige to be a faculty member is set by the policies of the educational institutions in awarding tokens of prestige. There might be some shift in the relative social status of different members of the faculty. But, if salary is taken to be an index of social standing, the indications are that few shifts would be necessary.

A theory based on prowess would also enjoy the benefit of a certain degree of historical continuity. Education among the Greeks consisted largely of competitive physical exercise, although a moderate appreciation of music was also considered appropriate in a gentleman. Of course, the Greek education would not, in modern terms, be considered an education at all, the Greeks in their primitive fashion refusing to award diplomas to any but the winners, but it ill behooves a promotional theory to be overly finicky in details.

The difficulty with this theory, however, crops up in another area. The notion of prowess is too close to the tangible. We have seen that the structure of the marketplace requires educational institutions to award tokens to ever-increasing numbers. Of necessity, a large proportion of these would be only moderately physically endowed. The Greeks solved this problem by practicing infanticide on those babies who failed to meet their rigorous standards, a practice which would engender protests if applied currently. In the absence of such latitude, educational institutions would be forced to manipulate the tests. For example, the broad jump could be measured with yardsticks suitably reduced from year to year, a practice not markedly different from present scorings. The necessity for constant use of tangible objects in the course of scoring would be bound to lead to occasional embarrassments, however.

Despite the handicap, educational theories based on prowess have maintained a *sub rosa* existence for many years. They remain a viable contender for the position of standard educational theory. Such a theory forms the basis for presidential pronouncements on the subject of education. Should the exigencies of the Cold War relax to the point where sizable government concern with the state of American education can be transformed into action, a prowess-based theory shows good possibilities of preempting the favorite position.

As of now, however, the standard theory is based on intellectual ability. Although intellectual ability is no more common in the population than prowess or prestiged lineage, the problems of recruiting faculties and students are technically well within the range of educational institutions, advantaged as they are by their right to set the criteria for prestige.

Actually, the theory is usually formulated in terms of the acquisition of knowledge. Since educational institutions take suitable precautions to hold constant the access to knowledge offered to students, as far as explanatory power goes the theory is indistinguishable from a theory based on intellectual ability. Nevertheless, formulation in terms of the acquisition of knowledge conveys the impression that anyone may benefit equally from education, making the theory a fortuitous choice in view of the institutional need to constantly increase enrollment. This distinction is not rigidly maintained, however, and if an occasional diplomate should enjoy the illusion that he has acquired intellectual ability in the course of his education, no one is much the worse.

Standard educational theory operates on the assumption that the acquisition of an education is an unequivocal good. Since the institution grants the student an education as a boon, a reasonable degree of gratitude on the student's part should prevent him from being unduly troublesome about trifles.[5] While, as our analysis indicates, the administration is not lacking in advantages in dealing with the students, the standard educational theory does contribute to a smooth-running institution.

The general assumption that education may be of advantage to anyone, implicit in standard educational theory, serves also as the ideological substructure for the notion that all should take part in the educational transaction. As we have seen, this notion effectively prevents the alumni from acting to raise the prestige level of the diploma. Again, the theory aids the administration in maintaining its position.

The advantages to the administration vis-à-vis students and alumni are, however, mere serendipitous by-products of standard educational theory. The framework of the theory is basically determined by the relationship to the philanthropic contributors, government and private, who supply the educational institutions' largest revenue. As we have suggested, the common notion of government motivation stems from classical economic theory, which takes the individuals' motivation to be self-interest and the government's to be altruistic. While the motivation of philanthropists is not organized into a theory, it is generally taken to be altruistic in nature. The educational institution thus sees itself as constantly in the position of having to cajole money from others whom it takes, on theoretical grounds, to be altruistically inclined.

It would, in the ordinary course of events, be passing difficult for anyone to ask for money on the basis that he likes money. For the person to say that he is in business to advance his own interests and would like another to contribute to his business in order to advance those interests still further would be equally naive. The educational institution must, of necessity, fall back on a theory that argues that it is in business for motives at least as altruistic as those credited to the contributor.

The educational institution must, therefore, say it is in business primarily to aid the spread of education. Of course, the administration and faculty get paid; but they must live. Being devoted to the spread of education, they then spend their efforts to see that their students acquire an education. But why do the students want an education? If the students are acquiring an education for their own benefit, the administration is in the position of working altruistically for the benefit of other self-interests. This, indeed, would hardly be a respectable position to take. It would make the administration look foolish. There is no choice, them, but to argue that the students also are engaged in education altruistically. The students are acquiring knowledge, not for their own benefit, but for the benefit of the community as a whole. The students, perhaps, are less aware of their altruism than the administrators are of theirs, but then this is to be expected of people with less sophistication. In any event, the students have comparatively little access to philanthropic sources, and their own peculiar views of the nature of education do not present a problem.

It would then follow from educational institutions' necessity for constant recourse to sources that they believe to be altruistic that the institutions must adopt something close to present educational theory. It seems to be characteristic of theory in general that it comes from educational institutions, or at least, from the products of educational institutions. Insofar as a theory has no connection with education, the amount of systematic buyers that can be expected from its origin is minimal. Insofar as the theory relates to education, the rather limited sources of theory have a decided effect. While a person can be quite cavalier about subjects with which he has no personal concern, it is rather a hardier individual who promulgates a theory that undermines the source of his income. By and large, educational theorists have been marvelously discreet in their treatment of this delicate matter.

It is commonly accepted that the educational institutions' major sources of revenue are altruistically motivated—and educational theory is based on this assumption—but it may be fruitful to examine this notion. Several of the theories that we have characterized as expositional, Downs's and Djilas's, for example, have taken the point of view that the government is run by men and that these men have interests of their own. In general these theorists have attempted to show how the interests of the members of the government form a system which is stable over reasonable amounts of time. From a purely theoretical point of view there is a certain elegance in attributing to the members of a government a motivation similar to that attributed to persons outside the government. From a purely empirical point of view such a contention would seem to be solidly grounded.

There has been rather less work done on private philanthropy. The preponderant number of analyses seem to be not entirely free from the tincture of personal interest. Vidich does suggest that philanthropists are not alone in rejecting self-interest, however. It is certain that the present tax structure is such that many individuals and corporations can express their altruistic desires at the government's expense rather than at their own. On occasion, philanthropic donations have left the giver somewhat richer than he would have been with less generosity.

All in all, there is good reason to suspect that the assumption of altruism on the part of philanthropists, government and private, does not faithfully reflect the facts of the matter. We should not, however, conclude that standard educational theory is misleading. On the contrary, one may reasonably conclude that a contributor, no matter what degree of self-interest prompts his contribution, is likely to be flattered by the notion he is behaving altruistically. Prudence suggests that a discreet reminder of the advantages of contributing be included. Once this is done, flattery, however fulsome, is unlikely to be wasted.

Notes

CHAPTER 1

1. For a description of medieval economics, see R. L. Heilbroner, *The Making of Economic Society* (Englewood Cliffs, N.J., Prentice Hall, Inc., 1962).
2. Adam Smith, *The Wealth of Nations* (New York, The Modern Library, 1937).
3. See J. K. Galbraith, *American Capitalism* (Boston, Houghton Mifflin Company, 1956), Chap. VI.
4. See, for example, N. Machiavelli, *The Prince* (New York, New American Library, 1952), Chap. XVIII.
5. F. Machlup, *The Economics of Sellers' Competition* (Baltimore, The Johns Hopkins Press, 1952).
6. W. F. Whyte, *Men at Work* (Homewood, Ill., Irwin-Dorsey Press, 1961).
7. Klee, *Surrender.*

CHAPTER 2

1. L. Coser, *The Functions of Social Conflict* (London, Collier-McMillan, Ltd., 1956), Proposition XV.
2. Smith, *The Wealth of Nations,* p. 128.
3. See H. Arendt, *The Origins of Totalitarianism* (Cleveland, The World Publishing Company, 1966).
4. A. Menen, *The Ramayana* (New York, Charles Scribner's Sons, 1954).

CHAPTER 3

1. James Duesenberry, *Income, Saving, and The Theory of Consumer Behavior* (Cambridge, Mass., Harvard University Press, 1952), pp. 25–32.
2. I. M. D. Little, *A Critique of Welfare Economics* (London, Oxford Press, 1960), p. 66.
3. "The meanest wretch puts an inestimable value upon himself, and the highest wish of the ambitious man is to have all the world, as to that particular, to his opinion . . ." B. Mandeville, *The Fable of the Bees* (New York, Capricorn Books, 1962), p. 48.
4. But see Aubrey Menen's introduction to *The Ramayana* for the argument that traits are, in fact, learned.

CHAPTER 4

1. C. H. Haskins, *The Rise of the Universities* (Ithaca, N. Y., Great Seal Books, 1957), p. 1.
2. *Ibid.*, p. 10.
3. See Albizu-Miranda, N. Matlin, H. Stanton, *The Successful Retardate* (San Juan, P.R., The Division of Vocational Rehabilitation, Department of Education, 1966), Chap. II.
4. E. H. Sutherland, *White Collar Crime* (New York, Dryden Press, 1949).
5. M. Nomad, *Apostles of Revolution* (New York, Collier Books, 1961), p. 11.
6. R. Flesch, *Why Johnny Can't Read* (New York, Popular Library, 1956).

CHAPTER 5

1. See the discussion of the cost of information in Anthony Downs, *An Economic Theory of Democracy* (New York, Harper & Row, 1957).

CHAPTER 6

1. The Opies report: Swotter, swotpot, stewpot, ant, bookworm, slave, plodderoner, and old grindstone. This should be considered as a representative, rather than an exhaustive, list. Also cited as common in certain circles is the couplet:

> He that works and does his best
> Gets the sack like all the rest.

Iona and Peter Opie, *The Lore and Language of Schoolchildren* (London, Oxford University Press, 1960), p. 179.

CHAPTER 7

1. For a discussion of zero sum games, see J. von Neumann and D. Morgenstern, *Theory of Games and Economic Behavior* (Princeton, Princeton University Press, 1953).
2. Duesenberry, *Income, Saving, and The Theory of Consumer Behavior*, pp. 25–32.
3. This theory is set forth in some detail and with much greater eloquence in Anthony Downs's *An Economic Theory of Democracy*.
4. See C. N. Parkinson, *Parkinson's Law and Other Studies in Administration* (Cambridge, Mass., The Riverside Press, 1957), Chap. I.
5. See the discussion of the division of labor in Smith, *The Wealth of Nations,* Chap. I.
6. *Ibid.,* Chap. X.

CHAPTER 8

1. B. Hoffman, *The Tyranny of Testing* (New York, The Crowell-Collier Press, 1962).
2. J. Barzun, *Teacher in America* (Garden City, N. Y., Doubleday & Company, Inc., 1954), Chap. XIII.
3. T. Caplow and R. J. McGee, *The Academic Marketplace* (New York, Basic Books, 1958), p. 114.
4. T. Veblen, *The Higher Learning in America* (New York, The Viking Press, Inc., 1918).

CHAPTER 9

1. F. Machlup, *The Economics of Sellers' Competition*.

CHAPTER 10

1. B. S. Phillips, *Sociology: Social Structure and Change* (in press).

CHAPTER 11

1. M. Djilas, *The New Class* (New York, Frederick A. Praeger, Praeger Paperbacks, 1957).
2. K. Mannheim, *Ideology and Utopia* (New York, Harcourt, Brace, 1955).
3. As a poetic recognition of this inherent limitation, we may cite Christopher Morley:

> When, as a child, I noticed
> That coal and ice were always sold
> By the same merchant
> I first suspected
> The irremedial duplicity of the world.

4. A. J. Liebling, *The Press* (New York, Ballantine Books, 1961), p. 4.
5. The general attitude of the administration toward students is summarized by Thomas Jefferson Tubb, Chairman of Mississippi's State Board of Trustees of Higher Learning, in commenting on the Chancery Court's reinstatement of an expelled student on the grounds that the University's expulsion had been based on unlawful search and seizure, "If the action of the court stands to the point where the university can't expel because of technicalities of defense that common criminals can demand, then the board of trustees and the institutions are in for a hard time in running decently disciplined places of learning." *The New York Times,* December 5, 1962.

Index